SEARCH FOR THE
MEANING
of LIFE

BRUCE & STAN

SEARCH FOR THE
MEANING
of LIFE

OUR TRIP ACROSS AMERICA

BRUCE BICKEL & STAN JANTZ

WORD PUBLISHING
NASHVILLE
A Thomas Nelson Company

Published by Word Publishing, a Thomas Nelson, Inc., Company, P.O. Box 141000, Nashville, Tennessee 37214 in association with the literary agency of Alive Communications, Inc., 7680 Goddard Street, Suite 200, Colorado Springs, CO 80920.

ISBN 0-8499-4237-3

Printed in the United States of America
1 2 3 4 5 6 QPV 05 04 03 02 01 00

CONTENTS

INTRODUCTION

Questions. Life is full of them.

Some questions arise from the deep recesses of your mind. You only have time to ponder them for an instant, stroke your chin, and say, "Hmmm." Then they suddenly disappear at your first distraction, never answered.

> **Question:** Why do they lock gas station bathrooms? Are they afraid someone will clean them?
>
> **Question:** If vegetarians eat vegetables, what do humanitarians eat?
>
> **Question:** If the cops arrest a mime, do they tell him he has the right to remain silent?

Other questions keep you awake at night. These are the gut-wrenching, nerve-racking questions that give the pharmaceutical companies big profits from the sale of antacid tablets and sleeping pills. You know the kinds of questions we're talking about: problems with your love life, your finances, or the upcoming performance review at work. (We don't need to give you any specific examples. You know what they are. And if you can't think of any right now, just wait until tonight.)

And there are a few questions—only a few—that have answers capable of changing your life. These are the big philosophical questions concerning your existence—such as, *Where did I come from? Why am I here? Where am I going?*—which can be summarized and synthesized into one overarching question:

WHAT IS THE MEANING OF LIFE?

· 1 ·

Many people think this is the world's most important question. Yet because it doesn't require an immediate answer, few of us take the time to work on it. At least we don't put it on the to-do list in our Palm Pilot:

7:00 A.M.	Breakfast meeting with J. P.
9:00 A.M.	Staff meeting
10:30 A.M.	Quarterly reports due
1:30 P.M.	Check out job site
5:00 P.M.	Work out
9:30 P.M.	Discover the meaning of life

No, this isn't how we approach it. We pretty much go through life with the meaning-of-life question nagging us from somewhere in the depths of our souls, but we don't really give the question the time or the attention it deserves.

Not too long ago, the two of us were just like you—overworked, over-committed, and overstressed. Then we realized that all of our overachieving wasn't getting us anywhere, at least not anywhere we wanted to be in five years. We decided it was time to slow down and take stock. We decided it was time to answer the world's most important question.

We decided to search for the meaning of life.

At first it seemed like a dumb idea. Who were we, a lawyer and a marketing guy, to answer a question that has eluded minds far more capable than ours (that pretty much includes the entire human race) for eons? But then this embryo of an idea started to grow. Before long, the single idea led to two distinct thoughts:

• First, we reflected on the rare and distinct privilege of ascertaining the myriad of answers to what might be the most perplexing query to confound the human psyche.

• Our second thought wasn't so sophisticated: *Road trip!*

This wasn't going to be just any road trip. We weren't going to find the meaning of life in a weekend in Atlanta. To uncover the answer to the world's most important question, we were going to have to take the road trip of a lifetime (at least of our lifetimes). We needed to travel across America!

As we began to plan our cross-country road trip, it wasn't the logistics that concerned us. Details of travel, scheduling, and cost were minor factors compared to the single greatest obstacle that stood in our way: getting permission from our wives. You see, we are two family guys with all of the accouterments (notice that we didn't say entanglements) that prevent most people from taking the type of expedition we were planning—a spouse, kids, mortgage payments, and jobs.

The alignment of the planets must have been just right, because when we pitched this idea, our wives heartily endorsed it. (The combination of Power Point and sock puppets also helped.) With our confidence brimming, we notified our respective clients that we were taking some time off to search for the meaning of life (we really said that, and they really bought it). Then we planned our basic route, did a wash, and hit the road.

As far as we know, we are the first two people in history to ever take such a journey. Many people have driven across America. Many people have searched for the meaning of life. But no one we have ever read about or encountered has done both.

By the time we were done, we had

- Driven over 10,000 miles
- Interviewed more than 1,000 people
- Traversed 30 states in 14 weeks
- Visited 11 major cities
- Asked only one question: "What is the meaning of life?"

While these statistics are accurate, they don't convey the entire spectrum of color and personality that characterized our trip. To get a sense of the flavor of our search, let us briefly tell you the *who, where, why,* and *what* of our search for the meaning of life.

WHO WE INTERVIEWED

We wanted to get responses from a cross-section of America, so we decided to interview anyone and everyone. From the rich and famous to the down and out. From the high and mighty to the lowly and meek. From the . . . oh, you get the idea.

We conducted on-the-street interviews in each city we visited, accosting unsuspecting pedestrians as we thrust a microphone in their faces (and only once did we misjudge the distance and cause dental damage). Don't get the wrong idea. We didn't limit our inquiry to strangers walking by. Sometimes we talked to strangers who were sitting still.

In each city, we identified a few key individuals we wanted to interview. We didn't personally know these people, so we had to rely on tenuous relationships to establish a connection with them. Actually, we were surprised that so many people graciously consented to be interviewed. Usually it was on the spur of the moment, or at most on short notice. Our interview list included university professors, professional athletes, families, politicians, construction workers, newlyweds, movie directors, entrepreneurs, retail clerks, clergy, atheists, college students, and lots more.

Many of our interviews were conducted in offices, but others were in much less conventional settings: an artist's studio, a southern mansion, taxi cabs, a golf course, a fish market, underneath an outdoor stage on Santa Monica beach, and a drive-through wedding chapel in Las Vegas. At first we took credit for our success in finding fascinating people in unusual places, but then we realized that we had nothing with it. It was the question that fascinated them.

WHERE WE WENT

A quest to find the meaning of life could have taken us to the far reaches of the globe, but our passports had expired, so we kept our search within the boundaries of the continental United States.

We started in Boston and drove down the East Coast, with prolonged stays in New York, Washington, and Orlando. From Florida we traveled across the South, hanging out mainly in New Orleans and Dallas. Then our search took us north through America's Heartland, past the *amber waves of grain* to St. Louis and Chicago. Next we traveled under the *spacious skies* of South Dakota, Montana, and Idaho until we crossed the Cascade Mountains (maybe not *purple mountain majesties,* but close to it) and reached Seattle. The last leg of our journey was down the West Coast, through Oregon, to the *fruited plains* of California, with stays in the Silicon Valley and Hollywood. Our trip ended in Las Vegas.

It was a search that took us from *sea to shining sea.* (There! All of the references from "America, The Beautiful." Can't you hear the orchestral chords crescendo in the background?)

WHY WE DID IT

Why did we leave our families and jobs for the summer and travel across the country interviewing people about the meaning of life? Because we were curious to know how people would answer this important question, and it is a question that relates to everyone. Ironically, it may be most relevant for people who think they have "no life."

We were fascinated by the prospect of talking with people all across the country to see if they had discovered the meaning of life. Think about it. If you knew how to answer the meaning-of-life question, you could:

- Put all of your problems and challenges into perspective
- Figure out what is important in life (so you can focus on that and not sweat about the rest)
- Live long and prosper

We were also excited because we had no idea what we would find. We had no preconceived notions about the types of answers we would hear. We didn't have a hidden agenda or an anticipated outcome. All we had was two blank notebooks, a clipboard, and some audio and video equipment.

Our interviews fell into a fairly predicable routine:

Step 1: Ask, "What is the meaning of life?"
Step 2: Listen to the answer
Step 3: Take notes

There were a few variations in the procedure that involved the fairly high-tech (for us) equipment we lugged with us: a minidisk recorder, a digital video camera, wireless microphones and headsets, and a laptop computer. We didn't know how to use all of this stuff, but we looked professional . . . at least until we took the equipment out of the case and had to find a twelve-year-old kid to help us get it working. Actually, we became fairly proficient with the equipment as time went on. By the end of our journey we could even use the wireless microphone transmitter on a belt clip without sending an electrical shock down our pants. (The limp in Stan's walk is hardly noticeable anymore.)

You'd have the wrong impression if you thought we just asked a question and got an answer. We did that, but it was much more than just Q & A. We actually had significant, substantive dialogue with more than one thousand individuals. Real people. Real conversations. Some of our discussions lasted for hours. (You'll understand why as you read the following chapters.)

These quality conversations were the unexpected reward of our search. At the outset, we didn't even imagine that we would hear such insightful responses. So, we can't say that these discussions were the reason we started the search. But they are certainly the reason we kept it going for the entire ten-thousand-mile journey.

WHAT WE FOUND

What we heard and learned on our search is the subject of the chapters that follow. But we will tell you this much right now:

THERE WASN'T JUST ONE CORRECT ANSWER TO THE MEANING-OF-LIFE QUESTION, BUT THERE WERE SEVERAL RECURRING THEMES IN THE RESPONSES.

As you can imagine, we heard a wide range of answers. Many of them were inspiring. A few were depressing. But mostly, the replies were unpredictable. For example:

• You'd be wrong if you thought that the question would be answered easily by anyone claiming to have a strong religious faith. We had some very interesting conversations with religious people, but some of them stumbled and fumbled on the question and had no ready response at all.

• You'd be wrong if you thought that people without spiritual faith are wandering aimlessly through life without any sense of meaning. We've got notepads and videotape full of enthusiastic responses from people who have no belief in God.

• You'd be wrong if you think that a lot of people responded with answers like "money" or "power" or "pleasure." We didn't get those kinds of answers. Maybe some of the people we interviewed actually believe that the meaning of life is all about acquiring wealth, but they didn't admit to it.

Before you start reading the chapters in this book, we need to make one important qualifying statement about our quantitative methodology: We didn't have one. We aren't anthropologists or sociologists. We are just cultural observers. So, our search was not scientific. Our findings won't qualify as data for a poll by George Gallup. But we think that's exactly what makes our search so interesting.

Our conclusions are based on anecdotal findings. We were dealing with real people, not cold statistics. There was nothing impersonal or sterile about our approach. (There was certainly nothing sterile about some of our motel rooms either, but we'll leave that story for later.) The answers we'll share with you in the next chapters evoked laughter and tears. People shared their hopes and dreams; they admitted their fears and failures; they shared from their hearts. You can't categorize those kinds of responses in a multiple-choice survey.

We hope this book encourages you to think about the question, "What is the meaning of life?" It is a question worth considering. Based on what we learned from our search, it seems to be a question that can actually change the character, quality, and direction of your life when you arrive at an answer.

BRUCE & STAN

One more thing. If this book motivates you to go on your own search for the meaning of life, we have one suggestion for you: If you are wearing a wireless microphone transmitter on your belt, don't stand in a puddle of water.

THE SEARCH BEGINS

Most of us do things in life that no one really notices, and that's OK. You don't expect special recognition for doing what you should be doing. You get up in the morning, take care of your hygiene routine, grab some breakfast at home or on the road, and go about your business. You don't expect people you see every day to greet you by saying, "Wow! You look fabulous! Your ability to groom yourself in such a becoming manner never ceases to amaze me."

You go to work or school, or you stay home and look after the kids. In other words, you do what everyone does—some days better than others—and even on those days when you achieve greatness, you aren't surprised that no one else notices. You're in a routine. You're doing what's expected.

Then there are those times when you step away from the ordinary and do something completely unexpected, at least for you. Perhaps you were inspired or motivated by another person, or maybe something inside of you said, "This time it's going to be different." So you interrupt the routine. You separate yourself from the crowd. You do something or plan to do something very significant, and you can't wait for others to hear about it.

You fantasize that your friends will stand back in amazement when they hear about your plan. Humility may be a virtue, but this is no time to hide your intentions. After all, people all around you will be impacted by your resolve. Lives will change as you carry out your idea. Others must know!

So you announce to everyone that you're going to Zimbabwe next summer to aid in starvation relief efforts, or you publicize your plan to lose weight, or you decide to train for the Tri-Cities Half-Marathon. Even better than all of these: You decide to search for the meaning of life.

"That's right, world. I'm going to do something very big. So what do you think?"

Here's where the cold, hard facts of reality slap you square in the face. Instead of jumping for joy, everyone just stands there. Rather than shaking their heads in amazement at your discipline, courage, and incredible dedication, your best friends try to refrain from yawning and respond, "I'm sorry. Did you just say something?"

Right then and there you've got a decision to make. Even though your grand plan could very well bring about world peace and end hunger as we know it, nobody seems to care. Do you bag the whole idea and go back to doing what's expected, or do you charge ahead anyway, regardless of who notices?

BRUCE & STAN'S BIG IDEA

If you can identify with any of this, then you know what we experienced when we first announced to anyone who would listen that we were going to take off three months to search for the meaning of life. So convinced were we that this was *the* idea of the new millennium, we began making plans for our journey as soon as we thought of it. We wrote out a proposal, mapped out a route, and set up a budget. It was the perfect plan, the ultimate quest. We were going to break new ground as we traveled across America searching for the answer to the world's most important question. It wouldn't be long before friends, strangers, and major corporations lined up to applaud us and offer to take care of virtually every need. The way we figured it

• A national car company would jump at the chance to give us a vehicle for our cross-country journey. *"Of course we don't mind driving this convertible sports car."*

• A prominent hotel chain would eagerly provide our lodging along the way. *"Oh please, the Presidential Suite seems unnecessary, but if you insist, we'll take it."*

• A well-known restaurant chain would gladly take care of all our meals and perhaps even sign us to an endorsement deal. *"Eat at Cracker Barrel, and tell 'em Bruce & Stan sent you!"*

• Several major Internet service providers would fight over the right to Web cast our tour. *"I'm trying to have a private moment. Is it necessary for that Web cam to be in here?"*

REALITY SMACKED US IN THE FACE

Oh, we had it all figured out. Such a lofty and noble cause would do no less than attract national sponsors and gain a worldwide following. But it wasn't to be. Like anyone else who runs a big idea up the flagpole of life and expects everyone to salute, we were disappointed (but not discouraged) when no one called. Despite our best efforts to explain our heroic cause to the right people, we didn't hear from any car companies, hotel chains, restaurants, or Internet companies. Even though the search for the meaning of life is the world's most important journey, all we got were a few puzzled looks and a lot of comments like, "Interesting . . . and you're sure people care about this issue?"

As a matter of fact, we do think people care. We thought so before we began our search, and we are fully convinced after finishing the journey. We weren't discouraged that our group of supporters—mainly our wives—wasn't bigger. And we did our best to accept the reality of our travel conditions.

• Instead of a free convertible sports car, we rented a sedan with high mileage. *"We didn't realize the Yugo came in this color."*

• Instead of luxury suites in four-star hotels, we settled for budget motels conveniently located near America's Interstate Highway System. *"Isn't America a great country? You see such a wide variety of landscape, people, and mutants."*

• Rather than dining in established eateries, we survived on convenience-store snacks and roadside fast food. *"You know, they say there's as much nutrition in two Twinkies as there is in a bag of sugar-coated Wheat Thins."*

• In place of a worldwide Internet deal, we built our own Web site. *"It's a good thing one of our sons knows how to do this. Does he know we're paying him with love?"*

Don't feel sorry for us. Not only did we survive, we thrived. Hey, you haven't experienced all life has to offer until you arrive in a complicated city like Boston with nothing but a reservation for some kind of subcompact and subhuman vehicle at Dirt-Cheap Rent-a-Car and a confirmation for one night at a number-named motel just thirty minutes from downtown.

BRUCE AND STAN'S ROAD MAP

1

BOSTON:

Can Knowledge Lead to the Truth of Life?

We decided to make Boston the first stop on our meaning-of-life tour for a couple of reasons. The first has to do with location. If you're going to go on a meaningful journey—one that will help a lot of people—it seems more logical to move from east to west than the other way around. Columbus went from east to west. So did Lewis and Clark. Even the sun rises in the east and travels west. So we figured, why not us? And if you're going to start in the East, it's best to start in the Northeast.

The other reason we started in Boston has to do with the city itself. Boston is a city of firsts. The first public school in America was founded in Boston in 1635. The following year Harvard, America's first college, was started. Boston hosted America's first full-scale tea party in 1773, and two years later, on April 19, 1775, the first shot in the Revolutionary War was fired in the Boston suburb of Lexington. In 1854 the first major free public library was founded in Boston, and the Boston Red Sox won the first World Series in 1903. (None of these things have been repeated since.)

What better place to begin our historical search than in a city of historical firsts and just plain old history. In fact, Boston is just plain old. We discovered this when we entered Boston's road and highway system, which for all practical purposes has not changed since the Revolutionary War.

There's a lot of talk in Boston about a massive highway project lovingly referred to as the Big Dig. This $11 billion public-works program was designed and launched decades ago (or so it seems—actually, it started in 1991) to clear up the congestion in downtown Boston by rerouting the freeways, toll ways, tunnels, bridges, and side streets—all at once. It's difficult to get a sense of the overall plan because the Big Dig isn't even close to completion. All you know is that when you leave Logan International Airport (especially when you're driving a rental car with 125,000 miles on it), you immediately realize you have problems for which there are no immediate solutions. Somehow we ended up on a ramp that took us skyward at a frightening rate, until we were on a one-lane road that circled what looked like a gigantic rock quarry.

Boston CityFacts

Boston

FOUNDED: 1630
CITY POPULATION: 555,447
GREATER BOSTON: 2,915,000
NICKNAME: Beantown
BUT WE CALL IT: Crummy Freeway Town
KNOWN FOR: Beans, crummy freeways, Red Sox, Bill Buckner, cod
FAMOUS NATIVES: Samuel Adams, Paul Revere, Benjamin Franklin, Oliver Wendell Holmes, Edgar Allen Poe, Jack Lemmon

In fact, that's what it is. In all of their wisdom, the Big Dig designers and contractors knew it would be impossible to get the big earth-moving equipment into Boston's city center each day, so they dropped a sand and gravel pit right in the middle of everything. As you drive through this lunar landscape, you see the picturesque Boston skyline on one side and this massive highway-making machine on the other. It's surreal.

WALKING THE FREEDOM TRAIL

As all visitors to Boston eventually do, we found our way to the historic city center. Even more impressively, we found a place to park. Once you've accomplished this, you can pretty much walk anywhere you want in less than thirty minutes. It's best to start at Boston Common, where you'll find the famous Freedom Trail.

We don't know who came up with the idea for the Freedom Trail, but we suspect that years ago the Boston Chamber of Commerce discovered a huge supply of red paint left over from marking all the "No Parking" curbs. They decided to paint a red line on the sidewalks and streets of Boston in front of such historic places as the Park Street Church, Benjamin Franklin's grave, and Larry Bird's shoes. (That's absolutely true—they bronzed a pair of Larry Legend's shoes and put them on the Freedom Trail.)

If you follow the Freedom Trail—also known as the Painted Red Line— you will see (among other things):

• The Old North Church, where lanterns warned the patriots that certain people wearing red jackets were on their way;

• The house of Paul Revere, the man who decided that lanterns weren't enough, so he rode through the streets of Boston on a horse yelling and screaming (Paul was the one yelling, not the horse, although Mr. Revere got hoarse);

• Faneuil Hall, where angry colonists used to meet before the Revolution (and where tourists from Iowa now buy trinkets made in China).

If you follow the Freedom Trail to its end, you eventually end up at Quincy Market, where you'll find many historic local restaurants, such as McDonald's, Dunkin' Donuts, and Subway. Actually, there are some real historic restaurants near Quincy Market, including America's oldest eatery, Ye Olde Union Oyster House. We ate there and enjoyed it very much, although we wondered if the photograph of Ben Franklin shucking an oyster was authentic. (Later, when we met Ben Franklin at Quincy Market and he charged us two dollars to take his picture, we knew the photograph was a fake.)

LOOKING FOR PEOPLE IN THE KNOW

By the end of our first day in Boston, we had visited just about every historic site the city had to offer. We knew it was time to do what we came to do: search for the meaning of life. And that meant talking to people. We were told by many Bostonians that we should look for the meaning of life at Boston's institutions of higher learning. We wondered why. Why just educational institutions? Why not in the homes, or in the churches, or even in the pubs of Boston? Why did so many people consider the colleges and universities to be the sole and exclusive repository of the answer to the meaning of life? Does knowledge give you an inside track to knowing the meaning of life?

We didn't intentionally start our search in Boston because of its educational emphasis. But Boston turned out to be the perfect place to start because it prides itself on being the capital of scholarship in the United States. With sixty-eight colleges and universities within the greater Boston area, it probably is. And, as we thought about it, it seemed to make sense: If you are looking for answers, start with the people who are educated. They might be the ones most likely to know.

NOWHERE ELSE BUT HARVARD

We found a list of institutions of higher education for Boston and the surrounding environs. At first glance, the list is intimidating, with names of such prestigious institutions as M.I.T., Northeastern University, Boston College, Brandeis University, and Wellesley included. But on further investigation, it became apparent that someone was stretching a bit to get the list up to sixty-eight. Some of those so-called colleges didn't consist of much more than a few students sitting around a table, talking about current events while they sipped cappuccino. (Where we come from, those places aren't referred to as colleges, but are called Starbucks.)

Bostonian As A Second Language

We don't like to stand out as tourists, so we tried to blend in as much as possible. At first we were worried about trying to fake a Boston accent. But very few people in Boston actually say things like, "I'm gonna pahk the cah in Hahvahd Yahd." It is the expressions more than the accent that are a dead giveaway of your sightseer status.

In case you ever go to Boston, here are a few of the rules for speaking the locals' lingo:

Rule #1: Abbreviate street names. Massachusetts Avenue is Mass Ave. Commonwealth Avenue is Comm Ave.

Rule #2: Abbreviate most everything else. You don't travel on the subway or the Massachusetts Bay Transit Authority or even the MBTA; you just take the T.

Rule #3: Don't outsmart yourself. Boston Common is called the Common, but the Public Garden is not called the Garden. If you say you are going to the Garden, you'll be immediately identified as a sacrilegious doofus: sacrilegious because the Garden is a reverential term reserved for the Boston Garden sports arena; and a doofus because the Garden was demolished about a decade ago and replaced by the Fleet Center.

If you follow these simple rules, you will significantly decrease your chances of being humiliated, mugged, or intentionally misdirected. You can thank us later.

We asked a few locals which of the real colleges and universities we should visit if we wanted to find the meaning of life. They all said that if you are searching for the meaning of life in Boston, you head one direction: away from Boston. But you don't go very far—just over the St. Charles River to Cambridge, Massachusetts, where you'll find Harvard University. Harvard was the place where the meaning of life would be found . . . if it could be found at all.

Smart people are presumed to have all of the answers to life. There is a special deference given to college-educated people by those who don't have much formal schooling. This fact became readily apparent to us when we interviewed people on the Harvard campus.

What Is Knowledge?

To look is one thing.
To see what you look at is another.
To understand what you see is a third.
To learn from what you understand is
   still something else.
But to act on what you learn is all that
   really matters, isn't it?
   —*Harvard Business Review*

It was a few days before graduation, so we decided to begin our on-the-street interviews by directing our microphones and notepads toward the guys setting up for the festivities. We thought these hard-working laborers would give us a good real-life contrast to the ivory-tower perspectives of professors and students. But they wouldn't respond. It wasn't that they were unfriendly. On the contrary, this was an obviously fun-loving group of guys, and they had opinions on everything from sports to politics to the economy. But when asked about the meaning of life, their replies went something like this:

"Don't ask us. We're just workers."

"We wouldn't know about something like that."

"You'll have to give that kind of question to the students . . . or the professors."

We got the hint.

ENCOUNTER WITH THE ERUDITE

As the guys on the Harvard work crew suggested, we caught up with a few professors. (They are easy to spot. They are anyone who isn't carrying a backpack.) To our surprise, the professors were rather befuddled when we asked about the meaning of life. One of them said: "I'm not sure there is a very clear meaning for me at this point."

As we talked to this professor further, he explained the role of education in ascertaining the meaning of life:

> **Professor:** Education helps give you the questions you need to find your way through the maze.

This comment blew us away. It meant we had been going about our search all backward by looking for *answers* to the meaning of life. According to him, *questions* are the secret to navigating through your existence. That professor must have been very effective at Harvard because most of the students we spoke with had lots of questions but very few answers. Maybe they were Harvard-equipped to make it through the maze, but they didn't seem very confident about it. Here are some representative responses from students to our meaning-of-life question:

> **Male student:** The meaning of life is getting away from Cambridge.
>
> **Female student:** I haven't got a clue about the meaning of life, but I wish I did.
>
> **Male student:** The meaning of life helps you decide what meaning is for you personally. But I don't know what it is.
>
> **Female student:** I never really thought about it before.

Those guys on the work crew were living under a huge misconception. All those well-educated professors and students had knowledge, but it hadn't led them to any ultimate truth about their existence. Their education apparently didn't translate into any tangible understanding about the meaning of life.

THE MEANING OF LIFE IS THE AMERICAN DREAM . . . OR NOT

Two students walked by as we were doing our interview shtick at Harvard. They appeared to be "a couple," and they both spoke about the meaning of life from a future, yet-to-be-attained perspective. We thought that was kind of cute—as if they were thinking of married life together. But we might have brought about the premature breakup of this potential marriage by causing them to realize their opposing viewpoints.

He said: "The meaning of life is 2.5 kids, a white picket fence, and a big American car."

After hearing his reply, she said: "The meaning of life is the opposite of whatever he said."

We hope that: (a) he was just being sarcastic; or (b) they get some serious premarital counseling.

NATURALISM IN THE SHADOW OF JOHN HARVARD

Harvard University is named after John Harvard. That's a huge honor for a guy who donated only two-hundred-dollars-worth of books to start the library. Of course, two hundred dollars was actually worth something back in the mid 1600s. Today that amount will hardly buy a textbook. There is a statue of John Harvard on the campus. It's a little bit like the statue in the Lincoln Memorial, only smaller (and without the beard).

We met an interesting couple sitting near the John Harvard statue. He had obtained his doctoral degree in applied physics from Harvard. She had an undergraduate degree from Oberlin College (in the less academic atmosphere of Ohio). They had been listening to some of our interviews and were eager to contribute their own perspectives. (Finally! Someone with a definitive answer.) While their answers were somewhat different, the theme of naturalism pervaded both.

Naturalism is the belief that natural causes alone are sufficient to explain everything that exists. In this philosophy, nature is all that exists—there is no God. The naturalist believes that life arose from the random, unplanned, and undirected collision of atoms; evolving through all stages and species of life forms into human life as we know it today.

Since naturalism presupposes no transcendent authority—such as God—there is no absolute truth, and all morality is relative and subject only to personal preference.

This was a delightful couple, and each of them was very articulate in presenting his or her perspective about the meaning of life. They had been married for thirty years, and their responses reflected a degree of life experience and maturity noticeably absent from the student responses:

She said: The meaning of life comes from enjoying it to the fullest. You should relish the world around you. Celebrate your children's success and their attempts at success. Enjoy this beautiful Earth with all the wonderful trees, grass, animals, and birds. Enjoy the wonderful stuff and let the rest of it go.

He said: The meaning of life is subsumed within the essence of who we are. The thing that uniquely defines us as *Homo sapiens* is our mind. Education can be an important part of what we do with that mind and what that mind becomes.

She added: All the learning that is really important happens after graduation, when you need and crave to learn something. When you come to Harvard, you aren't ready for this. Harvard opens your mind to all of the wonderful things there are in life, all of the dimensions in human learning. You are in a better position to relish and glory in all the wonderful things that exist.

This couple had enthusiasm and passion about life. Proponents of naturalism aren't always so vibrant and upbeat. Sometimes there is a sense of fatalism in people who adhere to the principles of naturalism, and we found an example just several hundred feet away. There we interviewed a Harvard premed major who was studying his organic chemistry text. He responded to our question about the meaning of life with this comment:

B&S Observation

IT IS OBVIOUS THAT MOST OF THE STUDENTS AT HARVARD DRINK FROM THE FOUNTAIN OF KNOWLEDGE. BUT APPARENTLY, A FEW ONLY GARGLE THERE.

He said: We're just animals. That's it. Just a step above the monkeys.

DOES TRUTH JUST FLAP IN THE WIND?

The Harvard campus had a majestic look when we were there. More than just the ever-present ivy-covered buildings, it had a dignified appearance because it was decorated for graduation. The most prominent of the displays were the gigantic banners hanging from the Widener Memorial Library building in Harvard Yard—colorful banners, each the size of Rhode Island, displaying the seal of Harvard University. The seal is emblazoned with one Latin word: *Veritas*. (For those who aren't fluent in Latin or aren't alumni of Harvard, *veritas* means "truth." We had to ask.)

We viewed the *Veritas* banners with awe for two reasons. First, they were spectacular—furling in the breeze as they hung between the columns of the grandiose library building. They looked so . . . academic. Second, this scene inspired us in our search for the meaning of life. Wasn't that what we were looking for in a sense? *Veritas.* We were on a search for the truth about life.

For centuries, the moral, philosophical, and religious beliefs of our country were based on the premise that truth was absolute. It was the truth of the Judeo-Christian beliefs. The truth of life could be found in the pages of the Bible. There was no doubting it. There was no disputing it. Society, as a whole, honored it. At its establishment in 1636, Harvard University was founded on the religious beliefs of the Puritans. John Harvard was a clergyman, and the first six presidents of Harvard were all members of the clergy. Even its motto proclaimed the existence of absolute truth.

The State of Education

Next to the District of Columbia, which isn't really a state, the Commonwealth of Massachusetts has the highest percentage of residents with a college degree. The state with the lowest percentage is Arkansas.

But a funny thing has happened to truth since Harvard was founded more than three and one-half centuries ago. In the twenty-first century, the predominant philosophy at Harvard is naturalism: a belief system that rejects the notion of God and of absolute truth. Even the statue of John Harvard is known as the "Statue of Three Lies." The inscription reads "John Harvard, Founder, 1638", but none of these three statements is true:

• No authentic pictures of John Harvard ever existed, so the figure seated in the statue is just some fictional guy;
• John Harvard was not the founder of Harvard College (although he was its first benefactor); and
• Harvard College was founded in 1636, not 1638.

What the early founders of Harvard considered to be the meaning of life—

a belief in God and adherence to his precepts—is now rejected as antiquated, irrational, and intolerant thinking. The naturalistic worldview is evident in the conversations with faculty and students, in the course catalogue, and in the required textbooks. This dichotomy has an impact on the search for the meaning of life. Either truth exists, or it doesn't. The Bible says there is truth and that the knowledge of it brings meaning to life. The essence of naturalism, on the other hand, would say that there is no meaning to life because there is no truth.

While on our travels, we came across a quote from noted biologist William Provine, who is on the faculty of Cornell University. He lectures extensively on the philosophical extensions of Darwinism, which is basically naturalism. Here is his succinct summation of the naturalistic worldview to which he subscribes:

No life after death.
No ultimate foundation for ethics.
No ultimate meaning of life.

Ouch! What does that mean to our search for the meaning of life? It occurred to us that the professor might be correct after all. We seemed to be accumulating more questions than answers.

EDUCATION, SUCCESS, AND THE BALANCE OF LIFE

We were ready for a break from the intellectual rigors of Harvard and the whole process of higher learning, so we headed west from Cambridge. We ended up in Watertown, a quaint town that has been transformed into a technology center. (You can tell because most of the warehouses that once housed industry have become offices.)

Due to the influence of Greater Boston's colleges and universities, this whole area is hot for high-tech. When the students graduate—especially students with entrepreneurial flair—they start businesses here, in much the same way Stanford and Berkeley graduates start businesses around California's Silicon Valley (see chapter 9).

We drove to Watertown to meet with a recent graduate of Babson College's M.B.A. entrepreneurship program. His name is Mark Johnson, and you could say he is living the American dream. While in his final year at Babson, Mark and two other students put together a business plan for a class—and for real. Before Mark and his colleagues graduated, they founded HighWired.com, an Internet company that helps high schools build Web sites. They were the first—and now the biggest—such company in the world, with more than thirteen thousand high schools around the world on-line. They have created a worldwide community of students who share news, ideas, and concerns with one another.

Mark is listed as cofounder and senior vice president of marketing for HighWired.com, but you'd never know that from his cramped office. He much prefers to move among his hundred-some employees, most of whom went to college in the Boston area. We asked Mark about the role education played in his current success.

Harvard Facts

Harvard is the oldest institution of higher learning in the United States. The first class had nine students; more than 18,000 students are currently enrolled. Harvard employs over 14,000 people, including 2,000 faculty. Six presidents of the United States were graduates of Harvard, and its faculty has produced more than thirty Nobel laureates.

"I believe that you need to go where the opportunities are, and for me that meant coming to Babson, which has built a phenomenal framework for taking people who have entrepreneurial traits and shaping them in a way that helps them evaluate which opportunities to pursue, and which ones to eliminate."

Mark came up with his great idea while still in graduate school. We asked him about the importance of great ideas.

"In this age, great ideas aren't what it's about. There are a lot of great ideas out there. In fact, there were probably a lot of folks thinking about our idea for HighWired.com at the same time we were. Where people should focus is not in the uniqueness of an idea, but the execution."

Mark talked passionately about his employees, and how important it is to add value and meaning to their lives.

"I am constantly reminded by our employees how much they enjoy working here. They love this partnership between the private sector of our company and the public sector of the schools we service. That's one level of quality of life we can offer. On another level, we want to be a fun business that offers people the opportunity to form relationships. We have a lot of activities, from bowling to baseball. It's great to have a hundred people wearing HighWired.com shirts going to a Red Sox game."

We had one more question for Mark. "At the end of the day, when you think about those things that really matter, where do you find meaning?"

"As a new father, the dynamics have changed. The pendulum has swung back to the nonwork-related life. But I'll be very candid. It's extremely difficult to find that balance between home life and work. I want to build a great company, but I also want to be a great father and a great husband. For me right now, the meaning of life is all about balance."

THE SOUL OF THE CITY

We were a bit reflective as we drove out of Boston. (With the traffic delays caused by the Big Dig, everyone has a chance to be reflective as they drive out of Boston.) We were impressed that it had all of the elements of a world class city.

• A sense of history: for Americans, three to four hundred years is about as historical as we can get.

• A sense of urban living: from brownstones to high-rise apartments, and the juxtaposition of the graveyard of the Old North Church with a Radio Shack nearby.

COLLEGE RIVALRIES

There are several bridges that cross the Charles River and connect Boston with Cambridge. One of them is called Harvard Bridge, and you can imagine that the students from rival colleges in Boston bristle at the mention of its name. Rather than deface the bridge, the eggheads at M.I.T. decided to calculate its length in units of measurement that would give their alma mater some distinction. In 1958, M.I.T. student Oliver Smoot laid flat and his classmates used him as a type of ruler, marking off the distance of the bridge in his body lengths. The bridge is 364.4 Smoots long (plus one ear). The Smootmarks are repainted each year.

• A sense of scholarship: throw a stone in any direction and you're likely to hit a professor.

While the city of Boston is mightily impressive, our thoughts on departure centered more on the abstract principals of freedom, truth, and meaning than on the concrete principles of history, urban living, and education.

FREEDOM

Here we were in the place where freedom in our country was practically born, yet not a single person mentioned freedom as a factor in the meaning of life. But as we thought about it, maybe that concept was an implicit element of every answer.

On the Harvard campus, all the people we interviewed enjoyed the freedom to pursue an education. That is a freedom that allows and encourages inquiry about life. And while Mark Johnson viewed balance as the meaning of life, we couldn't help but wonder if his answer would be different had he not been afforded the freedom to bring his creativity to the marketplace.

Even happiness as a meaning of life finds its fruition in the context of freedom. If "doing whatever makes you happy" is the meaning of life, then freedom is a necessary component. Without it, there is no "doing whatever."

TRUTH

We couldn't escape the mental picture of those *Veritas* banners flapping in the breeze at Harvard. We felt a little empty as we realized that many of the people we interviewed had no concept of a truth that never changes.

Our emptiness was soon overcome when we began leafing through a book we found (and paid for) at the Harvard Co-op. It's called *Finding God at Harvard*. Edited by Kelly Monroe, this recent bestseller features more than forty essays by "thinking Christians" who either attended or graduated from Harvard. Kelly attended Harvard Divinity School and later served as a chaplain to graduate students at Harvard. She began a lecture series called the Harvard Veritas Forum in order to bring people together who want to explore the original meaning behind the *Veritas* banners.

We looked through her excellent compilation and found some encouraging statements about truth, among them:

TRUTH IS NOT ONLY THAT WHICH AWAITS DISCOVERY BUT ALSO THAT WHICH WAS ONCE KNOWN BUT IS NOW THREATENED BY FORGETFULNESS. —ROBERT FONG

MEANING

Although we didn't walk away from Harvard with definitive answers, we weren't ready to admit that knowledge only brings more questions, or that truth is only what you make it. When you separate the natural world from the world of transcendent reality, as many people do these days, then life has meaning only to you personally, and not to the world as a whole. As our entrepreneurial friend Mark said, we must use our sense of balance to keep us on track. But is this enough? Do we have enough internally to give us meaning for the long haul?

Although we couldn't see it or prove it, we still had a sense that the truth is out there, and along with it meaning. And although you wouldn't know it by looking at us, we felt a little bit like agents Mulder and Scully. (We won't say which one of us is which.)

departure
00330

NEXT STOP: NEW YORK

2

NEW YORK:
The Culture of Life

It doesn't matter where you're from—the North, the South, the West Coast, or the East. You could be rich, poor, or somewhere in between. You may love the city or long for the wide-open spaces. But regardless of who you are, where you live, or what you've seen, you haven't lived until you've been to New York.

No tour book, travel guide, city map, or interactive Web site can adequately capture the concrete canyons, the crowded streets, the constant noise, the incredible intensity, the mind-boggling variety, the cultural fabric, or the in-your-face attitude that is New York.

We won't pretend that we can tell New York's story in a single chapter—no one can. But as we searched for the meaning of life in the world's most famous city, we had to go beneath the skin of the Big Apple in order to get to its core. (Go ahead, groan all you want.) That said, we quickly realized that you can't get to the core until you first see what's on the surface.

BUSTLING BOROUGHS

New York City is actually five separate counties called boroughs.

Queens is the biggest and, with nearly two million people, the second most populated borough. It is also the most ethnically diverse community in the world, which explains the colorful nature of Mets fans (Shea Stadium is in Queens). If you fly to New York, you will land in Queens, because both LaGuardia and John F. Kennedy Airports are here.

Brooklyn is the most populated borough with 2.3 million people. Brooklyn is famous for Coney Island and the Brooklyn Museum.

Staten Island, the least populated borough, isn't really known for much except for how you get there. You have to cross the Verrazano-Narrows Bridge or take the Staten Island Ferry; unless you live in New Jersey, in which case you've got your choice of four bridges (but they only go one way, because who wants to go to New Jersey?).

New York CityFacts

FOUNDED: 1625 (under the name of New Amsterdam; renamed New York in 1664 because the souvenir industry wanted a name with a little more pizzazz).
CITY POPULATION: Over 7 million. (It's hard to get an exact count because everyone is always bustling about.)
GREATER NEW YORK: 19,550,000
NICKNAME: The Big Apple
BUT WE CALL IT: The Big Bite out of your Wallet
KNOWN FOR: Wall Street; Empire State Building; Statue of Liberty; maniac cab drivers.
LOCAL HEROES: James Baldwin, Andy Warhol, Leonard Bernstein, Andrew Carnegie, and Casey Stengel.

Bronx is a largely residential community with the distinction of being the only borough on the American mainland (all the others are on islands). Yankee Stadium and the world-famous Bronx Zoo are here.

Manhattan, the smallest and most densely populated of the five boroughs, is easily the most well-known. To most people, Manhattan is New York, and for good reason. This thirty-one-square-mile island purchased by the Dutch for twenty-four dollars in 1626 from Native Americans is the heart of New York and the undisputed center of New York's cultural life. Whether you travel to New York to do business, shop, see a play, or take in the sights, you will definitely go to Manhattan (and you will probably stay there, just like we did, paying the equivalent of a month's salary for a hotel room the size of your closet at home).

BODACIOUS BUILDINGS

Manhattan has hundreds of famous skyscrapers and landmark buildings. The best-known skyscrapers are the Empire State Building (been there), the Chrysler Building (seen it), the twin towers of the World Trade Center (seen it), and Rockefeller Center (had lunch there). Landmarks you won't want to miss include St. John's Cathedral (the largest gothic cathedral in the world), Grand Central Station (very cool), Madison Square Garden (not even close to being square), and the Statue of Liberty (which proves the French can be nice).

Times Square, at the intersection of Broadway and 42nd Street, is another must-see landmark in Manhattan. All of New York's glitter, glamour, and grime come together at Times Square. The Theater District, along with all of those Broadway revivals so popular with tourists from Iowa, is right here.

SWARMING STREETS

There's one thing Des Moines—or any other city in America, for that matter—can't match: the streets of New York. We thought we were street smart after surviving Boston's colonial roads and the Big Dig, but Beantown is nothing compared to the Big Apple when it comes to urban hustle and bustle.

The first thing you notice is the traffic, but it's not the kind of traffic you're used to. In Des Moines traffic means there's a cow blocking cars on Route 16. In Los Angeles traffic is seven freeway lanes of vehicles averaging fifteen miles an hour. But in New York traffic is yellow, noisy, and unpredictable.

Yellow because most of the cars in Manhattan are cabs. The cabs are everywhere (except when you need one). And every single one of the cabs is noisy, because every single one is honking. For most people in America, a car horn is like your home smoke detector. It goes off only when someone's life is in danger. Not in New York. Here horns are an essential part of driving, like braking, only cabbies use their horns more than they brake.

Taxi Facts

There are 40,592 drivers registered to drive public vehicles in New York. These include street sweepers (used only after ticker-tape parades), cement mixers, and taxi cabs. There are 12,187 cabs registered by the Taxi & Limousine Commission. New York cabs are yellow Fords known as "Medallions."

—David Bradford, *Drive-By Shootings*

Which brings us to the unpredictable nature of New York traffic. Mostly it's congested and moving at a pace of one mile every forty-five minutes. Then there are those times when a rogue cab accelerates like a rocket because the driver has spotted an opening in traffic three blocks away. This actually happened to us, which caused us to think about the meaning of life in an entirely new way (mainly because our lives passed before us).

Because hailing a cab is practically a full-time job, most people walk in New York, which isn't all that unpleasant. Walking is good for you and relatively safe, as long as you look like you're very unhappy or mentally disturbed. If you're wearing a happy expression on your face (tourists from Iowa pay close attention), you risk being accosted by a mugger, or by someone selling Rolex watches for fifteen dollars (often it's the same guy).

COAGULATING CULTURES

"Melting Pot" seems like such a crude term. We prefer "blending bowl" (although "multicultural" is probably politically correct). However you say it, that's exactly what New York is. New York City has cultural richness that comes only from a genuine source: immigrants.

Even native New Yorkers aren't really that (unless they are of Native American Indian heritage). It just means that their ancestral roots go back farther—to the seventeenth-century Dutch and English settlers who established trade colonies in the New World. Since that early time, New York has been the main port of entry to the United States, and many of those who came didn't go beyond the city limits.

People were New York City's greatest import during the mid 1880s and into the early part of the twentieth century. In 1870, 83 percent of New Yorkers had at least one parent or grandparent born abroad. During the peak years of 1880 to 1910, 17 million people arrived in New York City from other countries.

An analysis of the immigrant phenomena of New York City invariably touches upon the meaning of life. That's because most of the immigrants were escaping political or economic oppression, and America was a symbol of hope. They endured great hardship for the dream of the American way of life.

• The first major immigration of Northern Italians came during the failing revolution in 1830–1840. Tough economic conditions in Southern Italy brought more immigrants in the 1870s.

• The potato famine in the 1840s was responsible for the influx of Irish immigrants. By 1860 they constituted one-quarter of the city's population.

• The African American population began to increase after the end of the civil war, and now Caribbean newcomers from Jamaica and Haiti are part of one of the fastest-growing immigrant groups.

• Russian persecution increased the size of the Jewish community in New York. By the start of World War I, there were six hundred thousand Jews living in the Lower East Side.

• The Puerto Rican population increased significantly shortly after World War II, and Cubans started to arrive in the 1960s.

• The last part of the twentieth century saw increased Asian immigration from Shanghai, Taiwan, and Hong Kong. With the Cantonese who arrived in the nineteenth century, New York's Chinese community is the largest in the United States (leaving San Francisco in the dust).

Each of these ethnic groups flourished and settled into communities within the city. There has been a sense of cultural pride in neighborhoods like Harlem, perhaps the best-known black community in the Western world; El Barrio, the vibrant Hispanic community; Yorkville, originally the uptown German district; and Hell's Kitchen, which was the first neighborhood for many Irish immigrants. These neighborhoods are in a constant state of ethnic flux, as when the borders blur between Chinatown and Little Italy. (So, when you have an authentic Chinese dinner and are still hungry, you can stop nearby and get genuine spumoni and a cappuccino for dessert.)

Merchant's Sign

We speak French, Italian, German, Jewish, Spanish, Slavic, Japanese, and all kinds of English.

All of this diversity brings with it a vast spectrum of opinion about the meaning of life. In matters of faith, for example, New York is a patchwork of religions with more than one hundred different denominations. (Catholicism is the most predominant; the Jewish community is the largest outside of Israel.) We felt intimidated and ill equipped to fully explore the meaning of life in New York City. After all, we spoke only one language between the two of us. (There are more than eighty official languages spoken in New York; the number of unofficial languages is equal to the number of cab drivers on duty.) This linguistic limitation just doesn't cut it when you are ferreting out the meaning of life.

We decided that we needed to find some kind of expert who could discuss with us the multicultural aspects of the meaning of life. But we didn't have a clue how to find such a person. And the yellow pages had no listings for "cultural counselor" or "sociological swami." (We did see a listing for an "ethnic escort," but we decided not to take a chance with that one.)

INTERVIEW WITH A CULTURE VULTURE

When a friend of ours recommended that we interview a man he described as a "culture vulture," we knew we had to meet this guy. Stan Oakes graciously invited us to meet him in his offices on the fifteenth floor of the Empire State Building, where he serves as the president of International Leadership University.

Oakes is fascinated by the dynamics of New York culture. That's just like us, in a way, except he has the mental horsepower to bring analytical insights into what he observes. We had a very casual conversation with him, but it was like sitting at the feet of a great philosopher. Using as many big words as we could think of to bolster our drooping end of the intellectual conversation, we asked for Oakes's insights on the meaning of life for three distinct groups:

Group #1: Members of the ethnic communities. We didn't want to miss this opportunity because we were fairly certain that we wouldn't be exposed to such culturally diverse neighborhoods driving through Nebraska.

Group #2: Recent immigrants. We wondered about the meaning of life for a person who has left everything to come to America. What is it in life that causes them to make such a drastic change?

Group #3: The Suits. We had a mental stereotype of the overachieving, hard-driving Wall Street executive types with high blood pressure and stress headaches. These are the intense men and women who make New York the only city where you have to worry about being run down on the sidewalk by another pedestrian. We thought this category might give us an interesting contrast on the meaning of life.

Acknowledging that his comments were generalizations in nature, Stan Oakes gave us the following perspectives:

GROUP #1: MEMBERS OF ETHNIC COMMUNITIES

The members of the ethnic communities within New York City often experience meaning in their lives through the celebration of their cultural traditions.

"For New Yorkers who are part of an ethnic community, a sense of identity and significance is found in national pride. You can see evidence of this in the rise of Latino and Puerto Rican music. That's part of the meaning of life for people. Aristotle called it 'love of one's own.' You have all this nationalism that is rising, especially since the fall of the Soviet Union. The whole city of New York benefits from this and participates in it."

GROUP #2: RECENT IMMIGRANTS

For many recent immigrants, the meaning of life comes through providing their children with opportunities that weren't available in the country they left.

"You have 400,000 Korean immigrants in this city. These parents are willing to sacrifice their entire lives for the sake of their children. They want them to be successful, so they pour their lives into them.

"They place a high value on coming to America, and there is a certain freshness that they bring—an appreciation of the freedom that the rest of us take for granted. For them, the meaning of life simply becomes living in America and just taking part in the American dream. They may work two jobs or have ten family members living in a one-room apartment, but they are willing to sacrifice their own personal meaning for the sake of their children."

GROUP #3: THE SUITS

Oakes explained some of the societal factors in New York City that impact people's perspective about the meaning of life.

Static. He wasn't talking about the crackling noise you get with poor cell-phone reception. He was referring to the busyness in everyone's life. Schedules are overbooked, and everyone is in a hurry. And there is too much information bombarding them from all available sources.

"While we have excitement for the technological advancements, it is producing an overload of information that is burying us. That fact is getting lost in the whole adulation of technology. Nietzsche had a great quote about the proliferation of information. Of course, this was back in the mid 1800s. He died in 1910. Nietzsche said that we need to be 'cold demons of knowledge' to separate out what is important."

Commuting. "When you work in New York City, where it takes you four hours to commute, you leave home at 7 A.M. and don't return until seven or eight or nine o'clock at night. You feel like a cow in a herd. It strips you of what is meaningful."

Personal Space. Most Americans enjoy a personal space of about three feet. This is the socially accepted "protected zone" that people aren't supposed to invade unless they have your permission. According to Oakes, New Yorkers don't have the luxury of a three-foot radius.

"In Manhattan, that personal space is reduced to three inches. Whether you are walking on the sidewalk or riding on the subway, people are going to be in your face."

Having explained the factors that contribute to the intensity of life in New York, Oakes began to probe the psyche of those corporate, success-oriented types. At the early stages of their careers, these men and women don't bother with anything of an introspective nature like the meaning of life.

"When they have just obtained their M.B.A.s, they are infatuated with the toys that wealth can obtain. And they use money to make life easier. Subsistence living in certain parts of New York City is $150,000 per year. The quest for success is so powerful that they don't allow themselves to ask the meaning-of-life question."

But all of this changes over time. As the years pass, they realize that their professional life has advanced at the expense of their personal life.

"For people of wealth, the meaning of life issues usually arise in the context of their families. They say things like:

I've become very successful, but I can't stay married.

This is my third marriage and it is falling apart.

My children don't love me; they hate me and don't respect me. They have no values, and no idea of what is right and good and true."

Bright Lights, Big Business

Broadway is more than a street in New York. It's big box office. Here are some statistics from *USA Today* for the most recent season:

Broadway attendance: *11.4 million*
Average ticket price: *$52.97*
Attendance of Broadway's touring shows: *11.65 million*
Total box-office receipts, including tours: *$1.2 billion*

This process of self-examination leads to a conclusion that life is empty and unfulfilling.

"They have a vacuum in their lives. Pascal called it a 'God-shaped vacuum.' Jesus Christ called it a 'thirst.' They don't know quite how to describe it because they have never before put words to their deep-seated feelings."

Since he brought up the references to God and Jesus Christ, we asked why more people don't find a solution to their emptiness through faith in God. His answer surprised us.

"The static and difficulty of life in New York City creates a lot of 'white noise.' People don't think they have time for God. Plus, there is suspicion that religion doesn't provide the answer."

Our conversation ended where it had started, as we talked about the many different religious views that are part of New York City's multicultural diversity. We mentioned to Oakes that New York residents do a good job of demonstrating tolerance to the rest of the nation. We thought we were going to impress him with our grasp of politically correct nomenclature. It impressed him, but not positively. How were we to know that he thinks tolerance is slightly deficient as a building block for society?

"I have never found tolerance all that fulfilling as a moral code. It doesn't require you to be proactive in your relationships. You can be indifferent and still be tolerant. But the Bible has a higher calling. God tells us to love our enemies. That requires more than tolerance. It requires establishing relationships with other people."

As we left the offices of the International Leadership University and traveled down the elevators of the Empire State Building, we realized that Stan Oakes knew more about the meaning of life than we could ever learn. We wondered if he was sitting at his desk thinking the same thing.

CONNOISSEURS OF CULTURE

We'll admit it. On our search, we read *USA Today* instead of the *New York Times,* but that's only because *USA Today* was offered free with our motel's complimentary continental breakfast (consisting of a banana and a granola bar). And we admit that when we're home, we watch *SportsCenter* instead of PBS. But despite all outward appearances, we are two connoisseurs of culture. And that makes New York City our kind of town.

Museums and Galleries. There are more than sixty museums in Manhattan alone, and about thirty more in the other boroughs. There are art galleries on every corner (next to the Dunkin' Donuts). We enjoyed our visits to the Metropolitan Museum of Art and the Guggenheim Museum. We got kicked out of the Museum of Modern Art because Stan kept trying to adjust the picture frames and Bruce sat on a sculpture he thought was an Ikea chair.

Theater. We aren't talking the cineplex that you find in any town large enough to have a stoplight. New York has big-time, legitimate theater. There's Broadway with all of the lavish musicals. These are attended by tourists from Iowa. New Yorkers go to the off-Broadway plays.

Concerts. Lincoln Center and Carnegie Hall are two of the most popular venues for concerts, ballets, and other fancy-smancy performances.

B&S Observation

HARVARD MAY PRIDE ITSELF ON PRODUCING THE LEADERS OF THE WORLD, BUT NEW YORK UNIVERSITY PRIDES ITSELF ON PRODUCING THE CULTURAL ARCHITECTS OF THE WORLD.

Literature and Publishing. New York is home to the major American publishing houses. Magazines published here include *Time, Vogue, Esquire, Vanity Fair, People, Ebony,* and *Rolling Stone.*

Television. The three major television networks are headquartered in NYC. That would be ABC, NBC, and MTV. Oh, and CBS is there too.

Fashion. The city is the fashion capital of America and a center for clothing design and manufacture. Some of the fashion designs we saw were so trendy that we can't tell you about them because they'll be passé by the time this book is in print.

The whole culture consciousness is so pervasive in New York, we figured it must somehow play into peoples' meaning of life. We felt compelled to seek out several individuals who were in the culture scene and ask them about it. So we hung out in the lobby of the W Hotel, where celebrities, the fashion elite, and other beautiful people of New York are seen. (We came in through the service entrance.) We approached a few supermodels with the line, "We'll tell you our meaning of life if you'll tell us yours." (Judging from their response, a guy's ability to construct a good pick-up line deteriorates in direct proportion to the number of years he's been married.)

ANNA AND THE DORKS

We did finally meet a young lady in the lobby of the W, so we didn't feel like complete losers. (Too bad she didn't share our self-assessment.) Her name was Anna, and she was a friend of a friend, so we all felt quite comfortable.

Anna is not a model, but she works in the New York fashion industry as a designer. She's married to an artist, so you could say that she is living the New York culture adventure, competing with other overachievers to make life work and to find meaning in it all.

As we struggled to find a comfortable position on the W's lobby furniture (burlap-covered logs carved in an Asian motif), we asked Anna the obvious question.

"This place is a glorified urban hell," she responded. "Everything in New York is difficult. The logistics of finding a place to live—a place you can afford—then doing everyday things everyone else in America takes for

Off Broadway With The Blue Man Group

To get an idea of the artistic off-Broadway theater scene, we went to the Astor Place Theatre in the East Village district to see the Blue Man Group's performance of *Tubes*. If you've seen the outstanding Blue Man Group show in Las Vegas (we saw that one too—see chapter 11), or the clever Blue Man Group commercials for Intel, then you know who these guys are. If not, imagine three guys dressed in black, only their shaved heads and bare hands are painted blue (not navy blue, not pale blue, more like a Smurf shade of blue). Their show consists of a lot of drum banging, marshmallow swallowing, and luminous paint splashing. It's wonderful! The grand finale involves the audience passing endless streams of toilet paper from the back of the auditorium to the front. We asked one of the Blue Man Group's stagehands to give us his meaning of life. (We talked to him through a tube connected from back stage to our seat.) Without hesitation, he answered: "Expression! We humans are the only cognitive beings capable of expressing themselves creatively. That's what the meaning of life is about!"

granted, like grocery shopping and transportation. All of this is very difficult. Opening a simple checking account is a nightmare."

"Is it possible to find meaning in New York?" we asked her, pencils poised. Anna took us seriously.

"I believe you have to break the meaning of life into fragments: relationships, success at work, the little things that happen in your day, and life lessons. The people I work with have a simple goal—to make a bunch of money. To me, that's the most meaningless purpose in the world." We could tell Anna had thought about our question, and we were impressed.

"Most people my age want more life experience. They want to travel. I grew up in the Philippines. I have traveled, and my husband has traveled. At this point in our lives we just want to get something done. We want to be more intentional about our lives, our relationships, and our work. I want to contribute to my field of fashion design, but more importantly, I want to help others. That's what is most fulfilling to me."

ON THE STEPS OF GRANDEUR

You can't hang out in the lobby of a chic New York hotel forever. The hors d'oeuvres in the lounge are so skimpy they wouldn't satisfy an anorexic. You just can't fill up on blanched beetle legs and barley husks served in a pecan shell. (Besides, those beetle legs get stuck in your teeth.) So, after our interview with Anna, we ventured outside in search of real food: a chili dog from a sidewalk cart.

If you try to eat your chili dog while walking on the crowded sidewalks of New York, you'll end up dropping the dog on the pavement and wearing the chili. You've got to sit while you eat. We chose the steps of the entrance to the Metropolitan Museum of Art. Step-sitting at the MMOA is favorite pastime of many New Yorkers. We used this opportunity to strike up a few conversations.

We spoke to Dennis, a first-year law student at City University of New York. He was quite articulate as he explained the role that museums play in the meaning of life for New Yorkers. (Law school hadn't yet raised him to higher levels of incoherence. That happens in the third year.) In addition to the obvious role of art exhibitions, Dennis said that museums contribute necessary components of:

• Space: The museums provide a spatial respite in the crowded city.

• Perspective: The very design of the buildings draws your vision upward. This is important in a city where everyone is always looking down at the sidewalk, avoiding eye contact with other pedestrians.

• Dialogue: New York may be the city that never sleeps, but it has a lot of residents that never speak. The museums foster expression of opinion and dialogue.

We were quite impressed with his erudite explanations. Then his girlfriend showed up. All of a sudden we wondered whether the museums really impacted Dennis's meaning of life or whether he just used them as a cheap date alternative. What he said made a lot of sense—and we believed what he was saying—but he might not have believed it. (He'll be a great lawyer someday.)

THE PORTRAIT OF AN ARTIST

Makoto Fujimura is a world-class artist living in New York. His unique Japanese style paintings are on display in galleries and museums around the world. His art was the focal point of the millennium exhibit for the Cathedral of St. John the Divine. Art critic Robert Kushner has called Fujimura's work "emotionally explosive." So what were we doing in Mako's studio? Good question. Call it the case of two guys discovering the meaning of life in the soul of an artist.

Our new friend Stan Oakes told us about Mako and his International Arts Movement (IAM), which seeks to unite artists with Christ-centered spiritual direction, promote creative excellence, and provide a forum for discussion and friendship, and he suggested that we visit Mako's studio on Greenwich Street. We figured we were going to one of those posh galleries in SoHo where people dressed in black gaze at artwork the rest of us can't quite figure out. Imagine our surprise when we met Mako, a very nice, very relatable young man whose art is absolutely stunning. We talked to him in his loft, an actual working studio with paints and canvasses and easels and all that art stuff.

We asked Mako about the art community in New York. "At the end of the 1980s," he said, "the bubble burst in the art community, and the artists lost faith in art. Because of the lack of an absolute foundation, people began to doubt if it was ever possible to create sincere expression, so the '90s became the decade of doubt. Now in the twenty-first century, there is general apathy. There is no cohesive meaning out there. The artists are trying to grab fragments of meaning, whether it's money, ideologies, or multiculturalism."

As we looked around Mako's studio, we saw paintings with vibrant color and deep texture (not bad for a couple of rubes, huh?). "Your work certainly doesn't look apathetic," we said. "It's visually stunning. How do you find meaning in your art?"

God's Masterpiece

Mako referred us to the book of Ephesians in the New Testament, where Paul wrote: "For we are God's masterpiece. He has created us anew in Christ Jesus, so that we can do the good things he planned for us long ago."

—*Ephesians 2:10*

"When I was studying in Japan," Mako continued, "I transferred my allegiance from Art to Christ. My vision was clarified. Whereas before I had an intellectual doubt of seeing reality as is, let alone depicting it, now my new-found faith gave me the foundation to see reality and trust it. Colors and forms I saw were indeed what others could see, and the objective world did connect to the subjective."

We were at the edge of our understanding, but we pressed on. "So you're saying that it is possible to express meaning through your artwork?"

"Absolutely. When your allegiance is to Christ, you embrace the biblical view of reality and you believe in the basic nature of communication. The power of what you express has meaning and significance in itself. An art student told me recently, 'You have something that you are convinced is true, and I find that refreshing.' I took that as a compliment, because you just don't see that in the art community."

We had one more question for Mako, and it had to do with the relationships he was building in the New York art community. "Will your greater impact come from your work or your relationships?"

"Unless I produce work worthy of my peers, I can't build relationships in the artistic community. Who you are in Christ and how you are valued by God is essential for understanding yourself. Out of that flows this point: your works express who you are. Then you must go into the community, into the world. The relationships are all there. If art is communication, then it is a bridge to create relationships."

THE SOUL OF THE CITY

We had a difficult time leaving New York. Literally. We have been in stop-and-go traffic on the freeways of Los Angeles, but that is not nearly as infuriating as being in gridlock in New York City. It took us over ninety minutes to drive two miles—and that doesn't count the twelve minutes Bruce spent trying to talk his way out of a traffic ticket for "blocking the box."

Everything is harder to do in New York. Especially the simple things, from grocery shopping to parking your car. And everything is much more expensive, from grocery shopping to parking your car. The tension and the financial pressure take a toll on people. Their lives are oppressively preoccupied with work and the anxieties of life.

We didn't see much smiling in New York City. We heard a lot of horn honking. And we saw a lot of extended middle fingers (especially when Bruce was blocking the box). Very few people were relaxed.

If there is a vacuum in people's lives, as Stan Oakes said, then the meaning of life must be whatever fills it. While New York creates an environment that intensifies the feeling of emptiness, it also provides some of the substance that fills the vacuum: pride and participation in cultural heritage; dreams for opportunity and success; and appreciation of the beauty and emotion of art and music.

And what about faith? Oakes quoted Jesus Christ as saying that we have an unquenchable thirst in our lives. Many New Yorkers, however, are skeptical of whether God can actually satisfy that thirst. But Mako Fujimura said that God not only filled his emptiness but also amplifies the emotion and meaning of his art.

We began to see a common theme in the comments we heard from the people we interviewed. They all mentioned, sometimes indirectly, an element that factored into their meaning of life: relationships. Did you notice it?

Stan Oakes talked about the wealthy who are saddened by their fractured relationships with their children. He talked about his personal conviction that tolerance doesn't foster the relationships that are developed when you follow the biblical mandate to love your enemies.

Anna said that she wants to be successful in the fashion field, but that she is more focused on being intentional about her relationships and helping others.

Dennis—our step-sitting, discount-dating friend—expressed appreciation for the conversations that are fostered by museums.

Mako left no doubt about it. "If art is communication, then it is a bridge to create relationships."

Maybe relationships are the substance that fill the vacuum in life. Maybe the meaning of life can be found in establishing friendships. Maybe the hard edge of New Yorkers could be softened with a kind word and a warm gesture. Maybe Bruce should have tried that with the traffic cop.

departure
00583

NEXT STOP: WASHINGTON, D.C.

3

arrival mileage

0 0 8 7 1

WASHINGTON, D.C.:
Living Between Power and Public Service

Arriving in Washington, D.C. can have a strange effect on an American. To someone from a foreign country it might seem just like any other U.S. city (only cleaner). But for U.S. citizens, this city is different because it represents those things that are distinctly American: the U.S. Constitution, a representative form of government, an independent judiciary, free speech, and sweaty tourists adorned in outlandish fashions with a cohesive stars-n-stripes motif.

As citizens of this great country, we felt a sense of ownership of Washington. This was our capital; these were our buildings; we owned this town. Actually, upon computing the aggregate amount of the federal taxes withheld from our respective paychecks over the years, we felt we had paid for a thing or two.

Washington, D.C. is the perfect choice for our nation's capital. There are so many patriotic monuments in the area. And with the White House there, the president doesn't have to travel very far to the Capitol to confer with the members of Congress.

With the patriotic sites so convenient, we couldn't resist the urge to visit them. We decided that the meaning of life could wait a bit because we wanted to get to the attractions before the lines of tourists got any longer.

We've got to be honest with you at this point. (Not that we haven't been honest before, but now we are going to be brutally honest.) We were a bit disappointed with all of the monuments. We didn't want to be. We are wholly patriotic, and we were even wearing outlandish fashions with a cohesive stars-n-stripes motif. But there were two factors that detracted from the magic of the moment.

First, the heat and humidity were so oppressive that even the statues were miserable. It wasn't just a hot day; it wasn't just the hottest day of the year; it was the hottest recorded temperature in Washington in the last hundred years. Our deodorant had worn off early in the day. We didn't care about offending the olfactory sensitivities of the other tourists, but we were even offending ourselves.

Capital or Capitol?

As the *Encarta World English Dictionary* explains, a *capital* is a town or city that is a seat of government, whereas a *capitol* is the building in which the legislature meets. The words would be used in a sentence as follows: Bruce & Stan were kicked out of the *capital* for carving their initials in the *Capitol*.

Second, many of the monuments were undergoing renovations of some sort. Either they were off limits or they were covered with all sorts of construction paraphernalia. The majestic aura of the Lincoln Memorial is lost with paint cans, ladders, and jackhammers lying around the monument. Maybe it was our own fault for coming during what is apparently the off-season when repair work is performed. How could the government be expected to anticipate that so many tourists would show up during the summer?

But we were not deterred by these distractions. We had grown accustomed to offensive smells because our rented sedan was from Dirt-Cheap Rent-A-Car. And we were oblivious to paint fumes and the rattle of jackhammers because we were staying at motels with numbers for names. Besides, we were good citizens, so we felt obligated to inspect the investment of tax dollars at all the major sites.

The Washington Monument. We couldn't get close-up because the construction crews had roped off the area. But this monument is best viewed from a distance anyway. It is a 555-foot tall obelisk. (Now we know what an obelisk is, but we still don't know what the monument is supposed to mean.)

The Lincoln Memorial. With great awe and anticipation, we walked up the steps of the classic Greek temple-like building that surrounds the statue of Abraham Lincoln. At the top we were greeted by surly tourists who were disappointed by what they had found. The Gettysburg Address inscribed on one of the marble walls was covered by a tarp. And there was construction scaffolding around the statue with cords from electrical drills dangling across Lincoln's face. (Apparently Abe's nostrils needed to be reamed and rebronzed.)

The White House. This has been the home to every U.S. president since the second, John Adams. They call it "America's Home," but the barricades, armed guards, and spiked fence convey the clear message that you aren't welcome to bring a hibachi on the front lawn or plop down on a La-Z-Boy in the Lincoln bedroom (unless you plan to make a sizable donation to the party in charge).

The U.S. Capitol Building. This has been the seat of Congress since 1800, and it is worth a visit. But learn from our mistake. You need an entry pass for the building, and make sure you get into the correct line. There are three of them. One is for a free, thirty-minute guided tour; one is for a self-guided tour; and one is for the rest rooms.

The Smithsonian Institution. Washington's most famous museum isn't just one museum; it is actually sixteen of them, plus the National Zoo. Our favorite was the Air & Space Museum where the exhibits are about things that fly: the Wright Brothers' *1903 Flyer,* Lindbergh's *Spirit of St. Louis,* the *Apollo 11* command module, and an IMAX documentary on Michael Jordan.

We designed our route through the monument maze so we would conclude with the Vietnam Veterans Memorial. Each of us had visited this site before, but it is always worth another visit, especially if you are thinking about the meaning of life. The names of the American soldiers who were killed or missing in the Vietnam War are inscribed in chronological order. The wall attracts more than 2.5 million visitors a year. Unlike the crowds at the other monuments, there was no shoving, no complaints here about the heat or humidity. People moved along the wall in silence. The things everyone was griping about a few minutes before suddenly seemed trivial.

A REARVIEW MIRROR PERSPECTIVE

Washington is a town where people are trained to speak in sound bites and to tell you what you want to hear. That was good news and bad news for us. Good news because those short sound-bite answers were easy to scribble in our notepads. Bad news because we weren't sure we would get honest answers.

As Chief Justice Rehnquist and the rest of the Supremes were on hiatus for the summer, we went to the next best source of objectivity we could think of: a taxicab driver. The cabby we talked to didn't hold back:

> EVERYONE WHO COMES TO THIS TOWN WANTS TO TAKE SOMETHING. MAYBE IT IS JUST FOR THEMSELVES. MAYBE IT IS FOR THEIR HOME DISTRICT. BUT THEY COME AND THEY TAKE.

We had no doubt about the truth of what she said when we got stuck with a $6.40 fare for a twelve-block ride. (She herself had mastered the "take" part.) But her comment made us wonder if everyone in Washington had an ulterior motive. Are the so-called public servants more interested in self-promotion than public service? This was a bigger question than the two of us could handle. We needed a staff of investigative reporters. But what are the chances that we could get a group of Washington journalists to sit around a conference table with us?

CHEWING THE FAT WITH THE JOURNALISM INTERNS

It is called the Summer Institute of Journalism. Each summer the program accepts about twenty college students, most of them editors of their college newspapers or top journalism students. The Institute is held in a three-story brownstone within walking distance of the Capitol. The students live in the apartments on the top two floors. Downstairs is a classroom, a large dining room and kitchen, and a conference room and library. The classes consist of lectures from some of the nation's leading newspaper reporters and others who are prominent in the news media. The assignments are simply stated but challenging: Find a story, write an article, and get it published.

We ate lunch with these journalism interns and their professors. Somehow, the topic turned to the meaning of life:

> THE MEANING OF LIFE IS LIVING EVERY DAY TO ITS FULLEST; IT IS SPREADING THE JOY IN OUR LIVES TO OTHER PEOPLE. WE MUST MAKE IT INFECTIOUS. —KRISTA FROM CALIFORNIA

MEANING COMES FROM THE PEOPLE IN MY LIFE AND THE RELATIONSHIPS THAT ARE A PART OF IT. —JODI FROM MINNESOTA

THE MEANING OF LIFE IS ALL ABOUT PERSEVERANCE AND HOW YOU HANDLE THE SITUATIONS YOU ENCOUNTER IN YOUR LIFE. IT'S ALL ABOUT ATTITUDE. — MICHAEL FROM TEXAS

We felt compelled to do a little investigative reporting of our own. Since we wanted to ask them if they thought politicians were genuinely service minded, we needed to find out if these college students knew what public service was all about. It didn't take long to be convinced that these students not only knew about it, but they also had a commitment to it.

HERE'S MY COLLEGE'S MOTTO: "TO SEEK TO LEARN IS TO SEEK TO SERVE." MY FRIENDS AND I ARE INVOLVED WITH BIG BROTHERS AND BIG SISTERS. WE REALLY ENJOY IT. THE BEST PART IS GIVING OF YOURSELF WITHOUT BEING PAID OR GETTING ANYTHING BACK. —RODNEY FROM OHIO

COLLEGE STUDENTS CAN BE VERY SELFISH. WE CAN GET WRAPPED UP IN OUR STUDIES. BUT YOU CAN MAKE TIME FOR COMMUNITY SERVICE IF YOU MAKE IT A PRIORITY. —LAURIE FROM OHIO

SOMETIMES IT IS DONE OUT OF A SENSE OF OBLIGATION. UNTIL YOU TURN IT INTO SOMETHING DONE IN LOVE, YOU AREN'T REALLY GOING TO GET THE TRUE EXPERIENCE OF WHAT IT MEANS TO SERVE SOMEONE. — MELISSA FROM MICHIGAN

YOU DON'T HAVE TO FEED FIVE THOUSAND; JUST FIND ONE FAMILY. BUT IT'S MORE THAN JUST HELPING THEM; YOU REALLY HAVE TO CARE ABOUT THEM. IF IT IS PART OF YOUR EVERYDAY LIFE, THEN IT WILL CHANGE YOU. — MICHAEL FROM TEXAS

OK, we established that these students had life experience in the subject of public service, probably much more than the Washington politicos.

After lunch, we met with eight of these students in their conference room for about an hour. They had been "on the beat" in Washington since the start of the summer, and we wanted to hear their impressions so far. What were the Washington elite really like? Specifically, we asked if these journalism interns had an opinion about whether politicians were in Washington to advance their careers or to do something good for society. The students were quite candid about the frustration and disillusionment that slaps you in the face in Washington. Here are some of their random responses:

> I THINK THAT MOST PEOPLE STAY IN POLITICS BECAUSE THEY BELIEVE IN THE ISSUES AND CARE DEEPLY ABOUT WHAT THEY SUPPORT. BUT LET'S ADMIT IT! LOTS OF PEOPLE ARE HERE BECAUSE THEY WANT THEIR NAMES IN PRINT.

> SOME PEOPLE ARE WORKING FOR JUSTICE AND TRUTH, BUT IT SEEMS LIKE EVERYONE ELSE IS OUT TO MAKE THEMSELVES LOOK BETTER. MAYBE THEY DO IT BECAUSE THEY THINK THEIR CAUSE IS IMPORTANT, OR MAYBE THEY JUST WANT THE LIMELIGHT.

> WE HAD A SPEAKER WHO SAID THIS ABOUT POLITICAL TYPES: "REMEMBER THAT THEY'RE REALLY NOT YOUR FRIEND." FROM A JOURNALIST'S PERSPECTIVE, I THINK A LOT OF PEOPLE IN THIS TOWN ARE TRYING TO BUILD RELA-TIONSHIPS TO ESTABLISH SOURCES FOR STORIES. A LOT OF THE RELATIONSHIPS ARE SUPERFICIAL, AND EVERYBODY KNOWS IT.

We left the Summer Institute of Journalism with mixed emotions. We were encouraged that there is student leadership in our colleges and universities that reflect lives of intelligence and compassion. But we were a little discouraged about the prospects of finding politicians who hadn't been sucked off the path of sincere public service by the forces of self-interest.

PRIVATE FAITH AND PUBLIC SERVICE

After a few days of interviewing students, touring Washington's monuments in the heat, battling the crush of summer tourists, and trying to interview lawmakers (students . . . heat . . . tourists . . . lawmakers . . . now there's a dangerous combination), we were ready for a little respite. When you're in need of a break from it all, a sanctuary is a very good place to go.

It was Sunday morning in Washington, and we decided to take our break by seeking out the sanctuary of the National Presbyterian Church, one of Washington's oldest. The concrete and stained-glass worship center and imposing bell tower aren't that old, but the heritage of National Pres goes back two hundred years and counts several U.S. presidents as past members. We didn't see any presidents, past or present, but we noticed plenty of young Washington professionals gathered together quietly, worshipfully, for the same reason as us. They were here to find refuge from the pace and noise of their lives.

Amazingly, Dr. Jeff McCrory, associate pastor of National Pres, delivered a stirring message on just that subject. "Our mind-boggling experiences are causing us to ask about spirituality," he said. "There is so much linguistic noise. How are we supposed to navigate this white-water romp through the spiritual rapids?"

Dr. McCrory had our attention. Then he focused on spirituality itself.

> Spirituality is about you and your singular relationship to God. There is a private focus to spirituality. I have my beliefs and you have yours. This is what postmodern spirituality is all about. But there is another kind of spirituality, and that's Pentecost spirituality, which has a public focus.[1] Pentecost spirituality causes us to engage the culture. It's a loud, public involvement in the marketplace. Is the church a place for peace and sanctuary? Yes. But it is also a place for raucous debate on life-and-death matters.

---

1. Pentecost was the day described in the New Testament (Acts 2) when the Holy Spirit came upon the disciples of Jesus and the community of believers, giving them the power to take the message of the gospel public. We happened to worship at National Pres on Pentecost Sunday.

As we left the sanctuary, we had questions. How do you engage the culture? What's the best way to get involved in the marketplace? How do you balance the private and public natures of spirituality, especially in a city like Washington? And what does all this have to do with public service and the meaning of life?

In our view, one of the people who best exemplifies this delicate balance of private spirituality and public service is Elizabeth Dole, former president of the American Red Cross, former secretary of labor, and former secretary of transportation. Oh yeah, and she's been a senator's wife as well. We bring up Mrs. Dole for two reasons. First, we happened to see her and Senator Bob Dole at National Pres that day. Second, we dug up a wonderful chapter written by Mrs. Dole in the book *Finding God at Harvard*. (She received a juris doctorate from Harvard Law School.) In it she describes her early struggle to engage the culture by engaging her faith. "I had God neatly compartmentalized, crammed into a crowded file drawer of my life, somewhere between 'gardening' and 'government.'"

Washington CityFacts

FOUNDED: 1790 (but the seat of government wasn't transferred from Philadelphia to Washington until 1800)
CITY POPULATION: 523,124
GREATER WASHINGTON: 4,563,000
NICKNAME: Home of the Nation's Capitol
BUT WE CALL IT: The Place that Spends our Nation's Capital
KNOWN FOR: Wind gusts and overheating (and that's just in Congress)
FAMOUS NATIVES: Duke Ellington, Goldie Hawn, J. Edgar Hoover, Queen Noor, John Philip Sousa
DID YOU KNOW? The District of Columbia was named for Christopher Columbus

Mrs. Dole then relates some insights gained from Gordon MacDonald on the story of Queen Esther.

As the Queen of Persia, Esther, a Jew, had access to the seat of power, but she was in a delicate position: Her husband the king didn't share her faith in God, yet she couldn't keep her beliefs private if she wanted to help her people. Esther wisely engaged her faith in God to prevent the annihilation of God's people throughout the entire kingdom. Without giving away the end of the story, we can give you the three insights, or themes as Mrs. Dole calls them:

Predicament. Esther was the Queen, but she was also Jewish. If the edict to kill the Jews was carried out, Esther would lose her position and possibly her life. Keeping her faith private was not the answer, yet going public was risky.

Privilege. God put Esther in a position to help his people, and hers too. If she didn't act, it was likely that God would find someone else to help. He always does.

Providence. One of the most stirring verses in the Bible is right here in Esther: "Who can say but that you have been elevated to the palace for just such a time as this?" (Esther 4:14).

Washington isn't a kingdom, and our nation doesn't have a king (at least we don't think so), but the lessons from Persia apply to the world of public service today. Thousands of people—some elected, some appointed, and others hired—come to Washington every year with the noble idea of impacting their communities, their states, and their nation for good. Most have a faith of some kind but are reluctant to share it with others. Others, like Elizabeth Dole, are looking for ways to engage their faith in the public square "for such a time as this."

> "The world is ripe and ready, I believe, for men and women . . . who recognize they are not immune from the predicaments of the day, who are willing to accept the privilege of obedience, and who are ready to see that the providence of God may have brought them to such a time as this."
>
> —Elizabeth Dole, *Finding God at Harvard*

Our discussions with the students at the Summer Institute of Journalism had made us skeptical about finding people in Washington with sincere and pure motives for helping others. But McCrory's message at National Pres and the examples of people like Elizabeth Dole made us believe that there were true public servants out there who were willing to engage their faith in the culture in order to serve the public. We just had to find them. And when we did, we were going to ask them questions like:

- Does your faith give you the motivation for public service?
- Is it possible to keep a balance between a vital private faith and effective public service?
- How do you find meaning in it all?

These are important questions because the answers have universal application. They apply to all of us, no matter what we do to serve others, whether it's in church, the soup kitchen, or our own neighborhoods.

THE TALE OF THREE STAFFERS

Washington is a town of young people. Not so much the politicians, but the staffers. (Even the "senior" staffers are usually under forty.) Some come during college for a semester's internship. Others move here after graduation from college or grad school. Some plan on returning to their home states after working in Washington for a few years. ("A year in Washington will look great on my resume.") Others end up making their careers in Washington.

We had a source in Washington who was connected with a network of these young professionals. We put in a request for the names and an introduction to several staffers who were well respected for their accomplishments and who were known to have a religious faith. Our source didn't fail us. It may cost us a Christmas gift basket as a thank you, but we learned a lot about the meaning of life from three Senate staffers (certainly worth the cost of a wicker basket filled with a few dried pears, several imported kiwis, and a bag of chocolate-covered raisins).

ZIAD S. OJACKLI

As the chief of staff for a U.S. senator, Ziad Ojackli is a busy man, but he had an aura of serenity about him. (He and his wife were expecting twins not long after our visit, so his life may be a little less serene now.)

He didn't strike us as a guy who was power-hungry or two-faced. He seemed genuine. So we asked him if people who come to Washington are really sincere about being public servants with a desire to help others.

"Absolutely. It is very heartening to see the number of people who care deeply about issues and are motivated by something other than the game or power. They care about education or health care, for example, and they want to make sure that their principles and faith are reflected in policy. Despite all the cynicism that exists, there are those who care deeply and are motivated by a higher purpose."

Because he alluded to spiritual matters, we asked him if his faith in God affected how he performs his role in government.

"There's no question that it does—on a daily basis. The integration of my faith into every aspect of my life is the most important thing. From your faith you get your principles. That faith must fit closely and dovetail with policy. It needs to be incorporated into the policies you pursue."

UNFAIR CAB FARES

After visiting so many major U.S. cities, we know a lot about cab fares. And they aren't as bad as we had expected. Except in Washington, D.C. Here, they are worse than we ever expected. It is like the fare system in Washington was developed by a committee of government bureaucrats. (Does that surprise you?)

In places like Boston and New York, the fare system is easy to compute. It is based on time and mileage. There are meters in each cab that click off the time and distance. When you reach your destination, you look at the meter and know the fare.

But not in Washington. Here fares are based on a myriad of unrelated and variable factors. For cab purposes, D.C. is divided into several zones. The fares appear to vary between zones, and there are extra charges if you drive across a zone boundary. So a trip of a quarter-mile within a zone is cheaper than a trip of only two blocks that crosses from one zone to another. Time and distance also appear to be factors, as you would expect, but it seemed to us that additional surcharges were assessed for: (a) riding while it was raining; (b) more than one passenger; (c) the use of windshield wipers in the rain; (d) honks of the horn; and (e) left turns.

Here's the biggest problem: There is no meter to show you the fare at the conclusion of your trip. And you can't compute it yourself (unless you are carrying a map, a ruler, a handheld scientific calculator with graphing capabilities, and a copy of the D.C. Metropolitan Transportation Code). Most confused passengers have no recourse but to just take the driver's word for it, pay the alleged fare, and get out quickly. (There are additional surcharges if you take too much time in exiting, or if each passenger exits from a separate door.)

The minimum cab fare within D.C. was $4.50. We decided it was cheaper for us to hail the cab, pay the $4.50 but not get in, and just walk to where we were going.

The journalism interns had obviously not met Ziad.

DENZEL E. McGUIRE

Those students hadn't met Denzel McGuire either. Denzel is the senior staff member for the Senate Subcommittee on Children and Families. This woman is so passionate about her job in Washington that her friends call her "On Fire McGuire." As two family guys with children back home (at least they were back home when we left on our search), we were glad to have someone like Denzel working in the government on behalf of families and children.

We asked Denzel how spiritual faith plays into lives of people engaged in the day-to-day battles of bipartisan politics.

"In Washington, people get passionate about their wins and their losses. Faith is an important thing because it serves as a good barometer—or balance—between passion and serenity. Faith allows you to know that whatever accomplishments you see here are part of God's plan. So, if you should not accomplish something one day or be disappointed because a particular bill does not pass, then having faith puts that in perspective. That result may be part of some bigger plan you're not aware of yet. It takes faith to have that viewpoint. It allows you to be passionate about your work but not so seriously that you put it above all else and let your work alone define you and your perspective."

We hadn't thought about faith in that context before, as counterbalancing passion to help you maintain the proper perspective. It made sense.

TOWNSEND LANGE McNITT

Even her name is impressive. It sounds like a Boston law firm. And Townsend's credentials aren't shabby either: an undergraduate degree from Gordon College, a volunteer stint at an orphanage in Zimbabwe, a law degree from Notre Dame, and special advocate appointed by the D.C. Superior Court to represent abused and neglected children. She is currently chief policy advisor for Senator Judd Gregg of New Hampshire.

Townsend is not shy about declaring the significance of her faith in God. "My meaning in life, more than anything else, comes from a passionate belief that Christians are called to engage in all different parts of society," she told us. "And government is just one of them. It is a tough one. And an exhausting one. But absolutely Christians need to be here in Washington. We need to be salt and light in the culture. If we were not here, then it would be a rougher place."

The people who know Townsend describe her as an accomplished and capable person whose faith is one of her defining characteristics. But the spiritual dimension of her life is not displayed in a way that offends others who have a different religious belief—or none at all. Like Ziad and Denzel, Townsend has managed to balance the private and public natures of spirituality in the fishbowl of Washington. All three of these brilliant people have done what Elizabeth Dole has done. They have refused to compartmentalize

How to Spot a Tourist in D.C.

Washington isn't a city as much as it is a working tourist attraction. In other words, at many sites the tourists are mixed in with the people who are trying to work. The Capitol Building is a good example. At any time, a hallway in the Capitol may be occupied by senators, representatives, staffers, FBI agents, government cafeteria workers, and a busload of visitors from the Serenity Now Retirement Villas in Palm Beach.

You might wonder how to distinguish the visitors from those who are working. (You wouldn't want to make an offhanded comment like, "I would kill for a glimpse of the president" if a Secret-Service agent was standing nearby.) Unfortunately, these government employees don't wear badges, but there is a simple way to identify the male tourists: they all wear short pants.

This is not just a phenomenon that occurs in the summer months in Washington. There is a universal truth that men on vacation, regardless of the place or the season, choose to wear pants that expose leg flesh from slightly above the knee to slightly above the ankle. (If male leg flesh has to be exposed, this portion is perhaps the least offensive.) Apparently men feel a sense of fashion frustration by the restraints of the working world, which require long pants. As we see it, if short pants are really that important for a guy, he should work for UPS.

God somewhere between the "gardening" and "government" files of their lives. Their vital private faith energizes their dedicated public service. We think America is better for it.

THE TALE OF THREE CONGRESSMEN

We've got to admit something to you. Working on Capitol Hill can be an ego-boosting experience. OK, so we weren't "working" in the sense of working to pass legislation or anything like that (aren't you relieved), but we were there walking the halls of Congress just like we belonged. The atmosphere is electric, historic, and more than a little awe-inspiring. Just a couple of days earlier we had wandered around Washington like the sweaty tourists we are, but now we were on a different level. It felt good (good enough to put on our ties and navy blazers).

After interviewing the Three Staffers, we decided to take it up a notch. Somehow we managed to get appointments with three congressmen in three different House office buildings. The person who arranged the meetings informed us that each representative had some kind of faith in God. Beyond that, we didn't know what to expect, so just like we had done with Ziad, Denzel, and Townsend, we prepared three questions to ask all three Congressmen:

- How do you intentionally integrate your faith into your work as an elected official?
- Have you personally found meaning here on Capitol Hill?
- What advice would you give to anyone who wants his or her life to count for something, whether it's in public service or anything else?

U. S. CONGRESSMAN JOHN THUNE

At first meeting, it's easy to see why the people of South Dakota have elected John Thune to Congress—he has the rare distinction of being his state's only House representative—with 75 percent of the vote in his last two races. He is very approachable and quite candid, and he had no trouble answering our questions.

"By its very nature, the political process is self-serving," he began. "By contrast, Christianity is all about self-sacrifice. So you basically have two kingdoms in conflict—the kingdom of self, and the kingdom of God, which calls for us to serve others. The Christian worldview should not be exclusive to the faith-based side of your life. We have a responsibility to be salt and light, to have an impact on our culture."

We could hardly take notes fast enough. Congressman Thune had thought this stuff through. Without skipping a beat, he told us how he finds his meaning in Washington.

"By keeping things in the proper perspective. The apostle Paul encouraged Christians to continue to believe the truth about God, and to stand firm in that belief. There is tremendous pressure on people today—especially young people—to be successful, but they lose perspective. So they look for success in money, fame, sex, and power. You see that here because people are looking for what they can get out of life for themselves rather than for what they can give back."

U.S. CONGRESSMAN CHARLES T. CANADY

We walked from Congressman Thune's office in the Longworth House Office Building to Charles Canady's office in the Rayburn Office Building. Congressman Canady was nearing the end of his fourth term as the House representative for Florida's 12th District. Rather than run again, he chose to serve as general counsel for Florida Governor Jeb Bush.

During his eight years in Congress, Canady got more done than most legislators get done in a career. He chaired a subcommittee, led the fight against racial preferences, and was the House sponsor of the Partial-Birth Abortion Ban Act. We were prepared for a short meeting with a busy guy, but instead we were drawn into a lively and informal conversation by someone who looked like he had all the time in the world for two strangers with note pads. (We were confident that our navy blazers helped.)

> "Mr. Canady is a walking rebuttal to the claim that careers in Congress must be long to be consequential."
> —*The Wall Street Journal*

"My faith informs my view of the world," Canady remarked. Then he came at our meaning-of-life question from an entirely different perspective. "My faith has an impact on what the questions are, not just the answers. In order to arrive at the right solutions, you have to ask the right questions. Meaning is found in question-asking and answer-finding, as long as you find the answers in those things that transcend individual circumstances. That's when you begin to get to the heart of what God's will is for us."

We asked Congressman Canady how he would advise anyone who wants to come to Washington to change the world. "Washington is like any other place," he responded. "People who come here with a noble calling are people who have the ability to be of service to the public. The key is having a servant's heart. God can work through people who are willing to get beyond themselves and serve others."

Hmmm. We were beginning to see a pattern here.

U.S. CONGRESSMAN THOMAS A. COBURN

Dr. Thomas Coburn is an intense guy. Maybe that's because, like Queen Esther, he really does deal with life-and-death issues. When we met him he represented Oklahoma's 2nd District, but he also represented the human race. That's because he is passionate about the rights of the unborn.

Congressman Coburn is an expert in this area. As a practicing physician specializing in family medicine and obstetrics, he has personally delivered 3,200 babies. As a congressman, he has played a central role in Medicare and health-care debates. More importantly, he has fought for legislation guaranteeing the constitutional rights of all human life, introducing a resolution recognizing these rights to the 106th Congress. "For thirty-five years, medical science has known that a human heartbeat is detectable twenty-four days after conception and that brain waves are detectable forty-one days after conception," he wrote. "If our laws respect the laws of nature in recognizing death, they must also respect the laws of nature in recognizing life."

Where does this passion and purpose come from? "For me, the meaning of life is wrapped up in the reality of who Jesus is," Coburn told us. He referred to a prayer of Jesus as recorded in John 17:3 in the New Testament: "And this is the way to have eternal life—to know you, the only true God, and Jesus Christ, the one you sent to earth."

Coburn continued. "Life becomes meaningful when you take what Jesus says and incorporate it into your life. The message of Jesus is the simplest in the world, but the most difficult to carry out. When you just talk about what Jesus said, it's easy to let your guard down. But when you live it, then others don't see religion coming; they see a life devoted to loving God and serving others."

As we left Congressman Coburn's office, he gave us one more thought. It pretty much summarized what we'd been hearing all day. "If you're willing to let go of any recognition of people, if you're willing to sacrifice yourself, then you can have a tremendous impact. That's what the courage of faith is all about."

FINDING LEADERS TO CHANGE THE WORLD

In the wake of our success on Capitol Hill, we decided to cast our Washington interview net a little farther. We had talked to students, staffers, and lawmakers. Now it was time to find someone in the diplomatic community. (OK, so we stumbled across rather than tracked down a real-live diplomat, but the effect was just the same.)

Dr. Robert Seiple isn't your typical diplomat. He is the former Ambassador-at-Large for International Religious Freedom in the Clinton administration. But when we caught up with him, Ambassador Seiple was in the process of forming a world-class think tank called the Institute for Global Engagement. Headquartered in Philadelphia, this organization is what is known in think-tank circles as an NGO, which stands for "non-governmental organization." It's also nonprofit (much like our own businesses back home would be by the time we returned to them).

"The Institute for Global Engagement has a Christ-centered mission and a global perspective. In my view, we have a missing generation of leaders because they had no leadership. Those who should have led insulated themselves inside their homes and careers instead of giving their all. This has to change. We need to find people who don't just want to do what's easy. We need to identify

> "If my faith isn't worth dying for, then it isn't worth living for."
> —Ambassador Robert Seiple

and challenge a new generation of leaders who want to change the world."

When Ambassador Seiple needed a chief operating officer for his international think tank, he knew he had the right person when he found Julie Peterson. Even though she is in her early thirties, Julie has traveled widely, doing her part to alleviate suffering in Third World countries. She has also worked on an executive level for a national nonprofit organization that helps prepare leaders for global service. We met with Julie in a hotel rooftop café overlooking several Washington landmarks, and we hadn't been with her for five minutes when she told us what she wanted as her epitaph:

THIS WOMAN DID NOT EXIST; SHE LIVED.

"Unless you are intentional about living, you just exist," she told us. "And as for this meaning-of-life schtick you guys are into, the answer is simple. Knowing an absolute God, and knowing that absolute truth exists, I must respond. My purpose and my meaning is to learn how to respond to that."

We asked Julie how she implemented that.

"First of all, to not be on the search for the meaning of life is the biggest mistake humans can make. Once you decide to begin your search, you need to do three things:

• Find out what the heart of God is all about. Make his passions your passions. Make his concerns your concerns. Tom Brokaw recently said, 'You can't win the world if you short circuit your soul.'

• Know yourself. How has God gifted you? Open yourself to all kinds of experiences.

• Understand the world and understand the way you need to fit in. We are not living in a vacuum."

During our earlier meeting with Dr. Seiple, he told us that he hired Julie as the C.O.O. of the Institute for Global Engagement because of her response to a single question: "What are your goals in life?" Her response was immediate: "I want to change the world." You know, we suspect that somewhere along the way, she's going to accomplish her goal.

THE SOUL OF THE CITY

Our notebooks were stuffed and our digital videotapes were full as we left Washington. We had met so many people and learned so much. Our search for the meaning of life was no longer a simple road trip. This was serious business. The students we interviewed showed us that they are already pursuing answers to the question of meaning. For them, meaning comes from relationships. Public service isn't just for public servants. We all must be intentional about serving others, realizing that the urge to serve doesn't come naturally. You have to work at it, but when you do, it changes you. (Note to us: We must never get to a point when we aren't around students. Their idealism and passion are great motivators.)

Just like the rest of us who form our opinions of Washington and politicians from the media, the students were skeptical about the political process (and this was before the most confusing and controversial national election in the history of our republic). Is it true that most politicians use public service like a gambler uses poker chips? Are they looking for anything beyond power and personal gain?

Had we not come to Washington to search for the meaning of life, we

WITHIN WALKING DISTANCE

A word of warning: You will be told that every monument and site in Washington, D.C. is "within walking distance." Don't believe it. Oh, that statement is technically true, but only if you happen to be standing next to it. Otherwise, distances on the tourist map of the Mall are deceptive and not to be trusted.

Just because you can see the Washington Monument from your current location doesn't mean that you can walk there within a day. It is 555 feet tall. It casts a shadow that goes all the way to Roanoke, Virginia.

And the Capitol Building always looks closer than it really is because it sits on top of a big hill. (Hence the phrase, "up on Capitol Hill.") Remember back to those art lessons in the third grade about perspective and depth of field. It will look close because it is big, but don't let that fool you. That sucker is far away.

We don't want to discourage you from walking around the capital. Hey, we are supporters of the prowalk movement (and we're fiscally conservative when it comes to paying those exorbitant taxi fares). We just think you should be forewarned. So, if you are going to walk from one end of the Mall to the other, carry a backpack with a change of clothes and enough food for several meals.

would have answered "yes" and "no" respectively to these questions. We would have believed that very little good comes out of Washington. But after digging beneath the surface, we found there is a soul of service seeping from beneath the veneer of power.

The soul of Washington has its origins in a deep faith that believes we must give ourselves to service. And when we are called upon, we need to stand up for the rights of all people, regardless of who they are and where they live. Just like there are many people in your community who believe this, there are many people in Washington—mostly people you've never heard of—who are there "for such a time as this." They know they are in a precarious position, but they believe God has put them there for a reason, and they count it a privilege. As our friend Ziad said: "Despite all the cynicism that exists, there are those who care deeply and are motivated by a higher purpose."

Now, we are aware that you may have some cynicism of your own at this point. You can accept that people of faith should be motivated to serve others (although you have seen plenty of so-called Christians who are as self-centered as they come). But what about those who aren't convinced that God is the answer (or even the question, for that matter)? Do they count? Do you have to have faith in God, or can you simply have faith in the goodness of people to serve others?

These are very good questions, and we must be very honest and tell you that we met many people in Washington and throughout our national search whose lives were dedicated to service, even though they weren't dedicated to God. We'll say it again more directly: Having faith in God isn't a prerequisite to service. You can find meaning in your life by seeking the good in others.

But is that all there is to meaning? Is the meaning of life all about loving and serving others, or is there more to it? Most of the people we interviewed in Washington seemed to think that God has to enter the equation at some point, but where? And how?

It's a good thing we're not done. We're just leaving the Northeast, heading south. The landscape is going to change, and we figure the people are going to change as well. Hang on as we find out.

departure
00951

NEXT STOP: ORLANDO

4

ORLANDO:
Living the Family Life

When you drive south along Interstate 4 through Central Florida toward Orlando, you can't help but wonder what this place was like before the Mouse arrived. It's a nice enough area, but there's nothing to distinguish it from any other region in the country dominated by swamps and forests. So you've got to ask yourself: Would all these houses, hotels, high-rise office buildings, world-class golf courses, and professional sports franchises be here if it weren't for Disney World?

The answer, of course, is no. If Walt Disney World—by far the biggest, most successful, and the most comprehensive tourist destination on the planet—were not right here, Orlando would be your average American city, only a lot more humid. But the fact is that Disney World is here, and Orlando is not your average American city. It is, unquestionably, the family capital of the world.

WALT DISNEY: FAMILY MAN

Before we get to the whole business of families, we need to tell you a little about Walt Disney, because without his vision for a first-class family entertainment center, parents would be dragging their kids to Coney Island or the Kansas State Fair rather than Disney World. "It all started when my daughters were very young, and I took them to amusement parks on Sunday," Disney once told his biographer, Bob Thomas. "I sat on a bench eating peanuts and looking around me. I said to myself, why can't there be a better place to take your children, where you can have fun together? Well, it took me about fifteen years to develop the idea" (*Walt Disney: An American Original,* Pocket Books).

The idea eventually became Disneyland, which opened in Anaheim, California in 1955. Walt Disney was already fifty-three years old, and a legend in Hollywood. He had moved there as a twenty-one-year-old with forty dollars in his pocket, hoping to make it as a cartoonist. Walt did more than make it. He single-handedly invented the animated cartoon, creating an industry that has entertained and influenced millions of children (for good and for bad) ever since. Every time you see a cartoon, an animated illustration, a video game, or anything that even comes close to resembling a Pokemon character, you should thank (or curse) Walt Disney.

Disneyland's success was immediate and enormous, but Walt regretted one thing. He had been able to purchase only 187 acres of Anaheim orange groves for his California land of enchantment, which left lots of room for cheesy motels and sleazy souvenir joints near the park's perimeter. That's why he was determined to find a lot more property for a second theme park somewhere in Florida. After extensive (and secret) research, Disney settled on Orlando. By 1965—before the locals were aware that anything was going on—the Walt Disney Company had purchased twenty-seven thousand acres of prime Orlando swampland for a total price of $5 million.

> "Disneyland isn't designed just for children. When does a person stop being a child? Can you say that a child is ever entirely eliminated from an adult? I believe that the right kind of entertainment can appeal to all persons, young or old. I want Disneyland to be a place where parents can bring their children—or come by themselves and still have a good time."
>
> —*Walt Disney*

Walt Disney died in 1966, but that didn't stop his vision from being carried out. Walt Disney World opened in 1971 with its first theme park, the Magic Kingdom (think Disneyland on steroids). That was followed in 1982 by the opening of EpCOT ("Experimental Prototype Community of Tomorrow," or as we found out after spending a day there, it can also mean "Every Person Comes Out Tired"). Disney-MGM Studios cut the grand-opening ribbon in 1989, and the fourth major theme park, Disney's Animal

Kingdom (which makes every other animal attraction in the country look like the hamster cage you had as a kid), first welcomed visitors in 1998.

Not Your Average Amusement Park

Walt Disney World currently encompasses forty-three square miles. That's roughly the size of Boston, and twice the size of the island of Manhattan. In addition to the four major theme parks, Disney World also includes three swimming theme parks; a botanical and zoological park; two massive entertainment areas; a sports complex; several golf courses, hotels, and campgrounds; almost a hundred restaurants; four navigable, interconnected lakes; a shopping complex; three convention centers; a nature preserve; a transportation system consisting of four-lane highways, monorails, busses, and boats; and a completely self-contained electric, water, and sewer system.

Disney employs more people on one site—between fifty-five and sixty thousand at peak times—than any other company in the U.S.

DISNEY WORLD: IT'S A FAMILY THING

We decided that our search for the meaning of life would be incomplete without a visit to the Magic Kingdom. After all, it is the "happiest place on earth," and if the meaning of life involves happiness, then this would be the place to find it. But we weren't counting on happiness being too great a factor (because the Florida humidity makes everyone irritable instead of happy). We really wanted to interview people about whether "the family" was part of the meaning to life.

Thirty minutes inside Disney World's Magic Kingdom was all we needed to confirm our belief that this was the place for families. Actually, we didn't have to be inside the park to get that impression. It was obvious during our ninety-five-minute ordeal to reach the front gate.

The day before we arrived, the Magic Kingdom had reached its maximum occupancy by 11 A.M., and the park was closed to incoming visitors by noon. If you were in the park by then, you were fine. But if you were just arriving (or if you had been in, gone out, and were returning) you were out of luck.

We weren't going to let that happen to us, so we arrived an hour before the park was scheduled to open. So did everyone else.

Like ants converging on the carcass of an elephant, cars from all directions flowed off the turnpike onto Disney World's private highway system. There was a slight delay at the entrance to the Magic Kingdom as people paid the parking fee and asked, "Is this the Magic Kingdom?" (as if the gargantuan entrance sign and attendants' uniforms were a hoax to divert traffic to Universal Studios). The line of cars then slowed to a snail's pace as we all parked with precise uniformity in a lot the size of Rhode Island.

Orlando CityFacts

Founded: 1875
City Population: 181,175
Greater Orlando: 1.4 million
Nickname: The City That Walt Built
But We Call It: Hot and Sticky Mickeyland
Known For: All things related to Disney World, and not much else
Famous Natives: We really couldn't find any, but we can tell you that Tiger Woods lives here

Once out of the cars, we waited for a tram that took us to a general staging/herding area where we converged with tram travelers from other regional parking zones. We were then allowed to make an independent decision: approach the main gate by train or boat or foot? (You see, the staging/herding area was still two miles away from the actual entrance.) We opted for the scenic water passage. More waiting before we could "come aboard." More waiting as the double-decker barge churned across lake. More waiting to disembark. Once ashore, all of the passengers raced to beat each other for a place in line where we waited some more.

We put these ninety-five minutes to good use by examining the people around us. And we continued our analysis of the vacationing visitors after we were finally inside the park. Most of them were families. Parents with children of all ages pervaded the entire place. The rest of us were definitely in the minority. (Being there without children certainly gave us a lot more freedom than the other adults who were fulfilling parental roles, but we also didn't have a kid to use as an excuse for riding through "It's a Small World.")

THE DISNEY EXPERIENCE APPEALS TO ALL TYPES OF FAMILIES . . .

It was easy to spot the families, but there was little in common among them. This was the broadest cross section of familial factions we had ever seen. Somehow, for some reason, Disney World appeals to all kinds of families. There is no single dominant group, class, or type that is attracted there. It has a universal allure to all families regardless of:

Shape. We aren't talking about body shape (although every possible anatomical configuration was present). We mean their apparent ability to endure the rigors of traversing the #1 tourist attraction in peak season. Some were obviously amusement-park veterans who came well prepared (parents equipped with cell phones and each child with a sonic transmitter). Others were inexperienced in theme-park excursions, but these novices were not intimidated by the magnitude of the Mouse house, though they came without a watch or a clue.

Size. Again, we aren't referring to skeletal dimensions or anatomical girth. We mean the number of family members. We saw some large family units, especially when you threw grandma and grandpa into the mix.

Economic Status. Here is where we expected to see a difference, because the exorbitant expenses at Disney World would seem to eliminate those of more modest means. But there wasn't any distinction. All strata of economic groups were prevalent.

Ethnicity. It wasn't like a PGA golf tournament where there is an underrepresentation of multicultural diversity. Disney World has an appeal for every cultural group. We heard dialects we couldn't identify or understand (and that was just with families from Boston and Dallas who were apparently speaking English).

Geography. Disney World's appeal is not just limited to American families. Many of the families were from foreign countries. They are identifiable because they speak with an accent that makes their English easier to understand than the families from Boston and Dallas.

... BUT THE LOGISTICS OF A DISNEY VACATION AREN'T FAMILY FRIENDLY

The longer we spent at the Magic Kingdom (we stayed until after the last fireworks display because we are conscientious cultural observers), the more intrigued we were by the affinity that families have for Disney World. We wanted to know why it has become the destination of choice for families around the world.

Disney's appeal for families becomes an even more amazing phenomenon when you consider the obstacles that a family must overcome to get there. Let's start with the most obvious difficulty: children (a key component in the family). Based on our observations, it is difficult to bring children to Disney World at any age.

Infants. It is surprising how many people bring their newborn babies to Disney World. Doesn't common sense dictate that if they don't have teeth, then they shouldn't come? (This rule should also apply to adults.) Parents struggled with strollers and diaper bags all day, and for what? The baby didn't know the difference between Mickey Mouse and the trash receptacle.

Preschoolers. These little critters have legs and know how to use them. Some parents tried to solve the problem of runaway children by using a restraining device they called a "boundary cord." (You would call it a leash.) For these parents, the day was spent unwinding the cord from the legs of irritated strangers. These children, fettered or not, were crying and whining most of the time. And by the end of the day, the parents were crying and whining too (because they spent $122 for stuffed toys and souvenirs for their child who was playing on the ground with a rock and a gum wrapper).

The Mouse That Roared

In addition to its theme-park and resort revenue, the Walt Disney Company generates income from an enormous media empire second only to Time Warner. Disney is a world leader in television and film production, broadcasting, publishing, music, and the Internet. In addition, Disney licenses more products than any other single brand, and its retail stores are found in virtually every mall in America.

Adolescents. If you pronounce it slowly, this age category sounds like "add less sense," which is exactly what it is. These kids were having fun, but they were constantly risking injury to themselves and liability to their parents. Whether it was trying to body slam Cinderella or flinging a fudgesicle at a float in the electrical parade, these kids were rambunctious.

Teenagers. It was easy to spot a teenager who was part of a family. It was the kid who was sitting relatively close to some adults but pretending not to know them. Another incriminating clue was that the kids rolled their eyes whenever the adults spoke. The kids wanted to be in Disney World, but not with the rest of the family. So, the parents spent most of the day trying to cajole participation from their teenager, and the teenagers spent most of the day trying to ditch their parents.

The hyperactivity of toddlers and the indifference of teenagers aren't the only deterrents to bringing an entire family to Disney World. The logistics of planning, scheduling, and implementing the trip for a family of five from Pittsburgh surpasses the synchronization required for launching the space shuttle. You've got to deal with arrangements for travel, lodging, meals, and potty stops. And despite the best of plans, you'll be confronted with unexpected delays, detours, and discouragements (like arriving by noon at Magic Kingdom after driving seventeen straight hours from Pittsburgh only to find out it closed five minutes earlier due to overcrowding).

And don't forget the greatest disincentive of all: the havoc that is wreaked on a family's finances. If our financial projections are correct, then most families who visit Disney World incur expenses equivalent to the tuition for two years at state college. ("We're sorry, son, but we can't afford to send you to college because we took that family vacation to Disney World five years ago.")

As we considered all of the obstacles and hardships that so many families were willing to endure for a Disney vacation, we became convinced that the whole Disney experience somehow played into the meaning of life for these families. We wanted to know why there was such a strong nexus between Disney World and families.

CONSULTING WITH THE CONSUMMATE FAMILY MAN

We were so intrigued by the importance that families placed on everything Disney, we broadened our investigation to include the other Disney venues. Over a period of three days, we hit the Magic Kingdom, Disney-MGM Studios, and EPCOT. (We skipped Disney's Animal Kingdom. Three days with all those families had given us our fill of beasts and other creatures.) With each passing day, we were increasingly convinced that the appeal of the Disney empire to families transcended mouse ears, water rides, and chocolate-covered frozen bananas on a stick. But our three-day Park Hopper pass had expired, and we still hadn't figured it out. Maybe we were delirious from the rides; maybe we were foggy from the fantasy of it all. We needed to talk to someone who could help us put it all into perspective.

We knew a guy by the name of Robert Wolgemuth who lived in Orlando. We thought he would be the perfect person to ask the question before us: Does the meaning of life come from your family? For one thing, as an Orlando resident, maybe he could explain why families are so mesmerized by the Disney mystique. More important, Robert has some impressive family credentials: (a) he has a wife (Bobbie), two daughters, two sons-in-law, and two grandchildren, so he's got practical, personal experience; (b) he is the best-selling author of two books about family life, *She Calls Me Daddy* and *Daddy @ Work,* and he wrote the commentary notes in the *Devotional Bible for Dads;* and (c) he owns Wolgemuth & Associates, a literary representation agency that works with several experts on family relationships.

We weren't disappointed with our choice. Robert had some great insights about how family plays into the meaning of life, and he gave us an interesting perspective on why Disney World is so popular with families.

QUALITIES OF A LEGEND

You can learn a lot from a guy like Walt Disney. What was it that made him the kind of person who could single-handedly transform the family-entertainment industry? Bob Thomas, Disney's biographer, listed three qualities:

Disney had an incredibly focused vision. The bright sharpness of his vision compelled those around him to achievement. Walt's vision infuses the company to this day.

Disney had an imperishable optimism that allowed him to overcome repeated failures.

Above all, Disney was a master storyteller, a quality that continues to impact the company. "The heart and soul of what we do is tell compelling stories," a high-level Disney executive was quoted recently as saying.

ON THE MEANING OF LIFE . . .

Robert explained the importance of the family comes from the pattern that God established.

First, the family is the paradigm that God chose to describe and illustrate our relationship with him. He is the heavenly Father and we are his children. There is something sacred about the family structure for God to use it so prominently. If it is that important to God, then it ought to be important to us.

Second, if we want to improve the relationships with our own families, we ought to study how God relates to us as members of his family.

And third, our impression of God shouldn't be as some distant, impersonal cosmic intelligence. We need to understand his fatherly characteristics and respond to him on that basis.

WHY DISNEY WORLD IS SO IMPORTANT TO FAMILIES . . .

Robert explained that Disney World provides each of its visitors (all 30 million each year) with the environment that they want—but don't have—in their family life.

Sanctuary. Many homes are not pleasant places. Oftentimes hostility is present. There is stress and pressures on parents and children alike. But never at Disney World. It is a safe environment where there are no cares or worries.

Joy and Laughter. In the sanctuary that Disney provides, families can laugh and have fun with each other. Disney is a place of joy. The entire Disney experience is crafted around humor. Disney World may offer the only opportunity for some families to laugh together.

Courtesy. Many families argue and fight more than guests on the *Jerry Springer Show*. Their homes lack any sense of civility or courtesy. Disney provides an escape from all of this animosity. Disney employees are taught to be gracious and kind; even the terminology used by Disney reflects this spirit of hospitality, as visitors are referred to as "guests."

Moral Values. Disney represents the moral values that people claim to have but that aren't really present in many families. "Clean" and "wholesome" are Disney trademarks. Families flock to Disney World for this environment.

A Sense of Togetherness. The hectic schedules of most families prevent them from spending time together. Seldom does the family participate in a common activity or even congregate in a common place. If the family is going to get together at all, it has to be out of town, where everyone is disconnected from their own routines. At Disney World, the family becomes cohesive because: (a) they don't know anyone else in the park to hang out with; and (b) the kids have to stick close to Mom and Dad because they have the cash.

As we discussed this family metaphor with Robert, everything came into focus. Families are attracted to Disney World because it offers, and delivers, the atmosphere that they want but often don't have in their homes. The fact that they go to such great efforts and expense to place themselves in the Disney environment indicates that they consider family to be a meaningful part of life.

ON THE ROAD AGAIN

After you spend a couple of hours with a guy like Robert Wolgemuth, you tend to get motivated. People like Robert are always thinking of new and better ways to do things, and they always challenge you to think.

We thanked Robert, got into our rental car, and drove west out of Orlando. It was time to digest everything we had learned about Disney World and families. As is our custom on the road, Bruce drove and Stan navigated. (We worked out this arrangement early on for two reasons. First, Bruce was born to drive. Some guys were born to be wild, others were born to run. Not Bruce. He is happiest when he's behind the wheel. Second, Bruce is unable to read the fine print on maps and computer navigating programs. About the only thing he can read is a large highway sign, since objects don't come into focus for him until they are at least fifteen feet away. So, for us to get anywhere—anywhere at all—Stan must navigate.)

B&S Observation

THE THREE MOST POPULAR DESTINATIONS ON THE PLANET ARE ROME, MECCA, AND DISNEY WORLD. ROME AND MECCA ARE EACH THE CAPITAL CITY OF A MAJOR WORLD RELIGION. AND IN A SENSE, THE SAME CAN BE SAID OF DISNEY WORLD. FAMILIES MAKE A SOJOURN TO ORLANDO TO FIND THE MYSTICAL QUALITIES OF LIFE THAT HAVE ELUDED THEM.

THE SOUL OF THE CITY

Orlando isn't so much a city as it is a portal to another world. We didn't find a soul in Orlando like we found in Boston, New York, or Washington. What we did find is a door to a place where family dreams come true—at least for a few days. For that reason, Orlando is in some world-class company: The faithful travel to Rome to visit the Vatican; pilgrims journey to Mecca to see the Al Haram mosque; and families go to Orlando to experience Disney World.

If there's a common thread we found among the families we watched and interviewed, it was their intentionality. Without exception, these families made detailed plans to come here, sometimes years in advance. They saved their money, coordinated their vacation days, and made their reservations just so they could wander through Walt's vision for a clean, fun, and friendly family place. They may leave their problems behind, and they may dread

LAYING A BRICK AT DISNEY WORLD

There is an expansive brick promenade that extends from the entrance at the Magic Kingdom around the lake to the neighboring Disney resorts. This boulevard is paved with the memories of families who have visited Disney World. Literally.

Each hexagonal-shaped brick is imprinted with the visitor's name, the date of the visit, and sometimes a brief message. It's a permanent shrine to memorialize the family's visit—capturing the memories in clay and mortar.

In shrewd business fashion, Disney has figured out a way to construct the promenade and make a profit in the process. It charges visitors for the privilege of buying a brick. (It's like purchasing your own star on the Hollywood Walk of Fame.)

Families are desperate to enjoy the Disney experience. With souvenirs, they can capture some of those memories and bring them back home. And now, for an additional charge, they can even leave a bit of themselves in the Disney dirt. The promenade is not yet fully subscribed. There is still time to have a brick with your name on it. Of course, after you go to Disney World and purchase a brick, then you'll have to make a return trek to worship at your hexagonal shrine annually until you die. (And maybe, for an additional charge, you can be cremated and have your ashes compressed into a brick so that you can be an integral part of Disney in perpetuity.)

returning to their hectic lives at home, but while they are here, these families come together to create meaningful experiences and magical memories.

Now all of this may seem a little idealized. We are aware that there are many critics who say that Disney's blatant commercialism and marketing manipulation are carefully designed to suck the soul out of the family while milking it dry. Disney World is fantasy, not reality. It doesn't do a thing to solve the problems eating away at families everywhere.

We acknowledge that Disney World isn't designed to put families back on track. If a family is fractured before going to Orlando, it's not going to heal after a few days in the Magic Kingdom. No, Disney World works best for families who are already on track. They are in the habit of carving out time for each other at home. An hour at the dinner table, an evening out, or a weekend away aren't rare occurrences but regular events that happen as a result of planning. A Disney vacation is just an extended (and much more expensive) version of what intentional families do all the time.

Disney Q & A

By far the most common question asked of Disney cast members is, "Where are the rest rooms?"

Our good friend and mentor John Trent has written extensively on the family and what it means to be intentional. John has a philosophy for families that can be summed up in two words: Be there. (In fact he has a book called *Be There!*) Here's how it goes:

Be there for your spouse. Being there is the opposite of taking from, which is what many married couples do, and that just doesn't work.

Be there for your kids. "Each child needs to hear he or she is chosen, imperfections and all," wrote John. "They need to know that Mom and Dad are proud their children wear the family name."

Be there for your friends. Here's a great quote: "What the eye of a friend sees, the heart of a friend moves to warm and encourage."

Be there for the world around you. This takes us back to our conversations with Townsend Lange McNitt and Denzel McGuire in Washington. They refused to isolate themselves inside the Beltway. They were there for the poor and the hurting in their world. We can't stay in Disney World forever. We have to be there for our neighbors and those who hurt in our communities. Here's how John put it: "Whose shoes need shining in your world today?"

When it was all said and done, and Orlando was just a faint image in our rearview mirror, here's what we concluded: Families don't give us meaning by accident. Families bring meaning to our lives because we bring meaning to them.

departure
02471

NEXT STOP: NEW ORLEANS

5

NEW ORLEANS:

A Passion for Life

As we left Orlando and headed for New Orleans, we weren't sure what we would find. Everything we had heard about New Orleans tweaked our interest. From what we had read, the city had a quaint mixture of French, Caribbean, and Southern cultures (everything from voodoo to mint juleps). But we wondered if this major U.S. city had become homogenized into American culture. Had it managed to retain its historical heritage and resist conforming to a franchise mentality? Or would it simply be a larger version of the New Orleans Square we had seen at Disney World (which was the same as every other part of the Magic Kingdom except for the architectural facades and the Disney music played in a Cajun style).

We drove past marshlands in the panhandle region of northwest Florida. There was no dirt to be seen on either side of the freeway. It was submerged under water with a floating layer of scum. In Florida, they use regular words to describe these areas. They are just plain old "swamps" or "everglades." But in Louisiana, they have their own unique way of describing the same thing. Louisiana doesn't have swamps and marshlands. (Well, they do, but they don't call them that.) Louisiana has "the bayou." That was our first clue that we were entering a land that time had forgotten.

WE'RE NOT IN AMERICA ANYMORE, TOTO

New Orleans is more like a foreign city than an American one. We aren't saying it should be expelled from the republic; it's just that there's no other place like it—not even close—in the United States.

Much of the city's uniqueness is glaringly evident. The street signs and business names use the letters from the English alphabet, but they aren't arranged in any order that is recognizable or pronounceable by anyone using words found in *the American Collegiate Dictionary* (and certainly not the *Oxford English Dictionary*). Other distinctions of New Orleans, such as the attitude and personality of the city, are only apparent as you talk to the people and absorb the city's culture.

It was obvious to us the uniqueness of New Orleans was authentic. It doesn't have to pretend to be different. It started out that way.

The French Influence. New Orleans was established in 1718 as a French settlement by Jean Baptiste Le Moyne de Bienville. (They couldn't name the city after him because they couldn't find a signboard long enough.) Back then it wasn't much more than a roughed-out clearing to honor the Duke of Orleans, Regent of France, who had claimed the entire Mississippi Valley for his country. With the Louisiana Purchase in 1803, New Orleans became a part of the United States. More precisely, we should say it was brought within the territorial boundaries of the United States. With residents who spoke French, worshiped as Catholics, and practiced voodoo, it wasn't really a *part* of the United States, and it surely didn't fit in with those Anglo-Saxon Protestants of the neighboring states.

Creole and Cajun: What's the Difference?

The Arcadians, whose ancestry is French-Canadian, eventually became known as Cajuns (it was easier to pronounce). Creoles are descended from French and Spanish settlers.

The French Canadian Influence. Beginning in 1605, there was a growing French community in the Arcadia region of eastern Canada. These Arcadians lived peacefully in the region for 150 years until a power-hungry English governor confiscated their land because they would not swear allegiance to the British crown. Many of these exiles began settling in New Orleans around 1765.

The Caribbean Influence. There used to be many plantations surrounding New Orleans. Slaves from the Caribbean region were housed in compounds at the mansions. The residents of these compounds eventually formed black communities. Fugitive slaves, called Maroons, lived in hiding with the Choctaw Indians in the swamps (oops, we mean "the bayou").

EASY, SLEAZY, AND OOZY

New Orleans is known as the Big Easy. It is a perfect description for this city that knows how to enjoy life. The ideal day for each resident would seem to include an extended stay on the patio at the Café du Monde, eating a beignet, sipping a café au lait, and reading the day's edition of the *Times-Picayune* newspaper. (We knew we had traveled far from Wall Street.)

A Big Easy attitude can run amuck if not given certain parameters. And the muck is found on Bourbon Street in the French Quarter. Every night of the year, Bourbon Street has a constant parade of revelers. It is an X-rated version of Disney World (with its own X-rated meaning for "Fantasyland"). The carousers are tourists for the most part, but it is the indigenous Big Easy attitude that promotes and sustains this debauchery.

New Orleans CityFacts

FOUNDED: 1718
CITY POPULATION: 465,538
GREATER NEW ORLEANS: 1.3 million
NICKNAME: The Big Easy
BUT WE CALL IT: The Big Sleazy
KNOWN FOR: Cajun music; Cajun cooking; Mardi Gras; booty shakin' on Bourbon Street
FAMOUS NATIVES: Louis Armstrong, Truman Capote, Harry Connick, Jr., Fats Domino, Bryant Gumbel, Al Hirt, Wynton Marsalis

The Big Easy attitude also impacts the city's appearance (and not in a positive way). Realtors would say that the downtown and French Quarter sections don't appear to have much "pride of ownership." We noticed a slimy substance oozing from every manhole. (We suspect that it has something to do with the fact that New Orleans sits at the end of the Mississippi River and receives whatever the thirty-three states and two Canadian provinces dump into the river upstream.)

A CITY OF PASSION

More than any other city in America, New Orleans assaults the senses. At least that's what we discovered as we searched for the meaning of life in the Big Easy. In New Orleans you *see* stuff you won't see anywhere else. You *hear* sounds unique in the world. The air is so thick with *odors* that your nose is constantly adjusting. Your *taste* buds dance in ways they never have before. And your hands can't help but *touch* the grittiness of a city that never comes clean.

As we filtered all the information coming though our senses, we tried to make sense of it all. What is New Orleans all about? Is it pleasure? Decadence? Expression? Excess? Individuality? Then it came to us. If there is one overriding theme that defines this place some call "The City That Care Forgot," it's *passion*.

GIVE ME THAT MAN
THAT IS NOT PASSION'S SLAVE, AND I WILL WEAR HIM
IN MY HEART'S CORE, AY, IN MY HEART OF HEART,
AS I DO THEE.
—WILLIAM SHAKESPEARE, HAMLET, ACT 3, SCENE 2

Passion has to do with your emotions and how you express them. Most of us work to control our emotions—love, joy, hatred, anger, stupidity—but New Orleans is a city that lets them all out. Some people equate passion with a strong sexual desire. Bingo. New Orleans openly offers objects of desire, and people come here from all over to do stuff they wouldn't dare do in their hometowns. Another definition of passion is "unbridled enthusiasm" for something. Now that hits the nail on the head in New Orleans. People here are passionate about—they have enthusiasm for—their city, their culture, and their celebrations.

A PASSION FOR THE CITY

The people of Boston are proud of their city, New Yorkers are arrogant about the Big Apple, and residents of Washington, D.C. appreciate their metropolis. But the citizens of New Orleans are passionate about their city. They love it in a way the rest of us love the special people in our lives. Visitors to New Orleans ask, "Who would want to live here?" The people of New Orleans declare, "We wouldn't want to live anywhere else."

If the infrastructure were falling apart and the opportunities were limited in any other city as they are in New Orleans, people would leave for greener pastures. Not here. They like it the way it is, glaring flaws and all. That's not to say that people haven't fled the city for suburban Metairie or the greener swamps of Florida, but those who have remained will articulately and passionately point out what they like about New Orleans.

HISTORY

No city has a more colorful and controversial history. New Orleans has seen it all, from world trade power to struggling seaport; from political power to political laughingstock; from nineteenth-century slave center to twenty-first-century melting pot. The French may have settled here first, but the Spanish took over, and today the city's black population is more than 60 percent of the total. Throughout the history of New Orleans, the Caribbean influence has infused everything. "We're more Caribbean than Southern," a student told us.

New Orleans has its share of families who have lived here for generations—sometimes in the same house. There's more old money than new. It's not death that people fear—they celebrate death—it's the loss of their history and traditions. The people of New Orleans are passionate about their heritage.

ARCHITECTURE

All of this history plays itself out in how New Orleans looks. One of the things that strikes you is the amazing architecture. The squares of New Orleans are richly textured beyond description. The most famous is Jackson Square, which sits in the heart of the French Quarter (another square). Across from Jackson Square is the two-hundred-year-old Saint Louis Cathedral. (Is it Gothic? Is it French? No, it's New Orleans!) Several square cemeteries—with their famous above-ground graves—dot the landscape.

Those famous New Orleans balconies with their fancy iron filigree, and the windows bordered by plantation shutters, create an atmosphere of romance and awe. The ornate nineteenth-century homes in the Garden District inspire a sense of history. Wherever you go you see the unique architecture and the unusual passion people have for preserving it.

LIFESTYLE

A lot of cities are tolerant of alternative lifestyles—San Francisco and Seattle come to mind—but New Orleans celebrates all kinds of behavior. The people here are passionate about preserving this freedom to express yourself, and people come from around the world to participate. You could say that in the case of New Orleans, one city's passion is everyone else's pleasure.

A PASSION FOR CULTURE

There are two basic types of culture. One type is enlightened and sophisticated. You acquire this kind of culture through education and the arts. This is what New York is all about. The second type of culture is more about the shared beliefs, values, and practices of a particular group of people. This is what New Orleans is all about.

Millions of people come to New Orleans to enjoy the city and revel in Mardi Gras, but there is a core of residents who define the culture by the things they believe and practice. Without these passionate people expressing themselves through their art, their food, and their language, New Orleans would be little more than a tourist trap. With them, the city is a world-class cultural center.

THE ARTS

New Orleans has a glorious history as a writer's colony. Mississippi native William Faulkner wrote his first novel here. Tennessee Williams wrote *A Streetcar Named Desire* while living in the French Quarter (you can almost here Brando crying, "Stella!"). There are plenty of art galleries in New Orleans, and when you walk along Royal Street, the antique stores seem more like history museums than shops.

Beyond the culture of literature and art is the strongest and best-known New Orleans cultural influence of all—music. But this isn't just any music; this is New Orleans music, and it's everywhere. Jazz, blues, rock, Dixieland, zydeco, techno, rave—they all flood the streets from the grimy little clubs of the French Quarter on any given night. You don't have to actually go in the clubs to listen (if it's after 10 P.M. the clubs are so crowded that you can't get in anyway); the music pours out through raised shutters and open windows.

Ask the locals (and we did), and they'll tell you the best music is played outside the French Quarter in little clubs or out in the open under wrought-iron balconies. We happened upon a three-piece blues band playing in the middle of the street for spare change. (They ran an orange extension cord from their little amp to a hardware store.) They were surprisingly good. If you're really serious about hearing all the great music New Orleans has to offer, come in the spring for the New Orleans Jazz and Heritage Festival, where the best local players and the world's best jazz, blues, and gospel musicians come together for a ten-day musical celebration.

A Brief History Of New Orleans Music

New Orleans is known as the City of Jazz for good reason. Jazz was birthed on the streets of New Orleans by blacks who picked up military instruments dumped after the Civil War. They blended traditional brass-band music with the rhythms of their African heritage. At the turn of the century, cornetist King Oliver more clearly defined the style of jazz known as New Orleans. He in turn apprenticed Louis Armstrong, the musician who eventually took the New Orleans sound mainstream.

Rock was born here too. Henry Roeland Byrd, aka Professor Longhair, developed a distinct style of rolling piano playing that influenced a generation of musicians, including Fats Domino, who added a touch of rhythm and blues. And you can't forget Dixieland jazz (we've tried, but we can't). Derived from King Oliver's influence, Dixieland is notable for its improvisational style, in which the instruments go off on their own—all at once. It's a fitting tribute to a culture of remarkable diversity.

THE FOOD

We made the mistake of walking through the French Quarter in the morning. Strolling down Bourbon Street in the morning is like walking through a frat house after a party. It stinks, there's garbage everywhere, and some guy on a bench is still "sleeping it off." We had dinner reservations in the French Quarter that night, and to be honest, after seeing things in the light of day, we were a little anxious. Not to worry. Tucked away in the nooks and crannies and courts of the French Quarter are several restaurants offering cuisine unmatched in any other city in the world. If you have the stomach to wade through the belching partiers on the street, you will be rewarded with a table in a courtyard and the eating experience of a lifetime. We ate in two four-star restaurants and several lesser-known eateries and cafés, and in each place, the people involved in preparing and serving the food had a clear passion for their craft.

THE LANGUAGE

We noticed a lot of different dialects as we traveled across America, but none are as distinct as New Orleanese, and no people are as protective of their native tongue as the inhabitants of New Orleans and Southern Louisiana. If you speak English, then you are at a disadvantage in New Orleans. Many of the local names and much of the local lingo is in French, or more correctly, Cajun. Even the English words are spoken with a dialect that makes them unrecognizable to most Americans.

Here is our Top-Ten-Terms list for New Orleans:

#1. New Orleans: Never, we repeat, never pronounce the name of the city as "noo-or-leens." And don't pronounce it any other way that requires three syllables. Say it all in one syllable to sound like *N'awlins*.

#2. The French Quarter: Although you'll see it listed in all of the tourist books, local residents won't know what you're talking about if you ask for directions to "the French Quarter." If you want to get there, you better say it so they understand it. Tell them you're looking for *da Franch Kwatas*.

#3. Gumbo: This is a local dietary mainstay—a hearty soup mixture of chicken, seafood, and vegetables—not to be confused with the green clay-mation figure known as Gumby.

#4. Po-Boy: This is a popular meat and cheese sandwich, not a penniless male child.

#5. Beignets: This is the famous New Orleans-style donut-type powdery sugar thing. Your visit to the Big Easy won't be complete unless you eat one of these, so you better learn to pronounce it correctly: it's *bin-YAY*.

#6. Tchoupitoulas: The main thoroughfare through the warehouse district leading to the French Quarter is pronounced *Chop-a-TOOL-us*. (Say it three times silently to yourself before you say it out loud to the cab driver.)

#7. Lovebugs: Don't let the name fool you. They are annoying, sticky insects.

#8. Banquette: You'll be disappointed if you are expecting an all-you-can-eat buffet. It's a sidewalk.

#9. Café au Lait: Be forewarned. Don't expect what they serve you at those upscale Yankee coffee cafés like Starbucks. You're in Cajun country. Be prepared for the taste of chicory.

#10. Mo Bettah: The progression of superlatives goes like this:

Good	=	Good
Better	=	Bettah
Best	=	Mo Bettah

A PASSION FOR CELEBRATION

New Orleans is a city of non-stop celebration. There are parades for funerals, holidays, and religious observances. Depending on the time of year, there is the New Orleans Jazz and Heritage Festival, the Spring Fiesta, and the New Orleans Food Festival. Saint Patrick's Day, Saint Joseph's Day, and All Saints Day are celebrated here with gusto and passion. And then there's Mardi Gras, the granddaddy of all celebrations. Granted, a lot of the celebrators are drunken frat-types and wanton women from out of town, but the true spirit of celebration runs deep and has its roots in a strong spiritual base.

CELEBRATING RELIGION

This is a heavily Catholic area as evidenced by the many churches, festivals, and celebrations. The Pope even made a stop here a few years back. Crowding in on the Roman Catholic tradition is a very real voodoo presence. This isn't some playful version of the real deal. This is the real deal. A slave uprising in Haiti in the 1790s brought an influx of West Indian blacks to New Orleans, and they brought with them their voodoo religious rites.

The French Quarter is littered with voodoo shops, and you'll find voodoo fortunetellers out in the open. We were walking through Jackson Square, and we noticed a voodoo woman reading someone's palm, right there in the shadow of Saint Louis Cathedral. From a safe distance (we thought) we lifted our camera to take a picture. Even before the shutter clicked, the woman glared at us and promised to curse us unless we took care of her (translation: slip her a couple of bucks). Not wanting to take any chances, we paid the woman, who released her curse and posed for our photo. (We're not making any of this up.)

A couple of blocks from Jackson Square, at the corner of Bourbon Street and St. Peter Street, we noticed a man holding a large wooden cross. This was a high-tech cross, because on the horizontal beam there was an electronic sign (the kind where red letters scroll the message from right to left) that read: "Jesus loves you . . . but He hates your sin . . . "

CELEBRATING MARDI GRAS

You don't think of the world's most hedonistic, blatantly sinful celebration as a religious celebration, but that's exactly what Mardi Gras is. Now, we aren't so naïve as to think that those who engage in the decadent behavior that characterizes Mardi Gras believe they are participating in a religious event, but the roots of this celebration are definitely spiritual.

Mardi Gras (French for "Fat Tuesday") is the holiday before Ash Wednesday, and it always falls between February 3 and March 9. Ash Wednesday marks the beginning of Lent, a period of fasting and penitence traditionally observed by Christians in preparation for Easter. In other words, Mardi Gras is the last time to indulge in food and drink (translation: get wasted and eat yourself stupid) before the temperance of Lent.

The people of New Orleans are passionate about Mardi Gras, and so is everyone else. From its humble beginnings in 1857, Mardi Gras in New Orleans has grown to a $1 billion annual event that attracts upwards of three million people.

More Mardi Gras

Mardi Gras in New Orleans is the most famous pre-Lenten celebration of its kind in North America, but the tradition is carried out around the world, where it is known as Carnival.

The biggest Carnival events are held in Nice, France; Cologne, Germany; and Rio de Janeiro, Brazil.

PASSIONATE PEOPLE

We realized very quickly that we couldn't get to the heart of the meaning of life in New Orleans simply by eating the food, listening to the music, and watching the drunks on Bourbon Street. As we had done in each place we stopped, we needed to find the people who defined the city and its theme by the meaning they were bringing to their lives.

We didn't find any college presidents, ambassadors, political professionals, or family experts. In fact, we didn't find anyone. For the most part, they found us. And they turned out to be some of the most fascinating people of our entire journey.

ALEX: SUPPLYING THE PASSION

As previously mentioned, we frequently ducked into restaurants to avoid the ooze and the odors of New Orleans. Or at least that was our excuse.

We had an interesting discussion with Alex, the owner of one restaurant.

It was a French restaurant (big surprise), and he was from France (equally big surprise). We talked with him about the struggles of owning and operating a restaurant. We discussed the enthusiasm he has for all aspects of the culinary arts—from preparation to presentation.

Because we had been thinking about the issue of passion while we were in New Orleans, we directed the conversation that way. "So, we guess it is fair to say that food is your passion," one of us said. His reply surprised us. "Not really. Art is my passion. I would much rather be painting than standing in the kitchen. The restaurant is the way I earn my living."

A Bite of Beignets

They call it the New Orleans version of a donut, so we were expecting something between a Dunkin' Donut (on the low end) and a Krispy Kreme (on the high end). But it's not like a donut at all:

- It's not round.
- It doesn't have a hole in the middle.
- And it doesn't come in an unlimited variety of styles or frostings, or even with the option of those little sprinkle things on top.

About the only similarity to a donut is that the New Orleans police officers eat a lot of them.

We're talking about the *beignet,* a triangular shaped hunk of deep-fried dough covered with powdered sugar. It is delicious when served warm. And it is even better when joined by a cup of coffee.

Eating a beignet is every bit as palate-pleasing as consuming a Krispy Kreme, but dispel from your mind any notion that they are similar:

- Unlike the airy, cotton candy-like texture of the Krispy Kreme donut, the Beignet goes down easy but then lands in your stomach with a thud;
- A Krispy Kreme will leave your fingers sticky for a few hours, but with the Beignets you'll be brushing powered sugar off your face and clothes for the rest of the day; and
- Eating four or five Krispy Kremes at one sitting will leave you feeling stuffed, but eating four or five beignets will leave you dead.

Then he taught us an interesting lesson about passion. Knowing that the restaurant business is a demanding job that allows little free time to the owner, we asked him how often he gets away from the restaurant to focus exclusively on his artwork. "Very seldom," he said. We gave the obligatory, "Oh, that's too bad" response. "Not really," he shot back. "You see," Alex went on, "I bring my artwork into my restaurant."

We glanced around the room looking for an easel, a canvas, and some brushes, or at least one of the paintings on the wall with his autograph. But that isn't what he meant. "I try to be artistic in all aspects of this restaurant. Instead of separating my love of art from the restaurant, I incorporate the two of them. Whether it is selecting the artwork for the walls, or how I set the tables, or the presentation of the food on the plate, I am being an artist." Then he said something so profound that we had to stop chewing so we could think about it:

"I DON'T LIVE FOR MY PASSIONS. I LIVE THOUGH THEM."

Then Alex rushed away to attend to a restaurant emergency (some flambé fiasco). We were relieved that he had to go, because we needed a few minutes to whisper between ourselves about what he had just said. We knew it was profound, but we weren't sure what it meant.

We think Alex was making the point that he doesn't work a job and then, on rare occasions, find a moment to enjoy his art. Rather, he found a way to bring what he is passionate about into his everyday life. He has arranged his perspective and the circumstances of his life so that he infuses passion into his regular routine.

Alex supplies passion at his restaurant. You can see it all around, but it's not on the menu (although that wouldn't be out of the realm of possibility for a restaurant near Bourbon Street).

KERRY: SHARING A PASSION

Not far from our hotel was Mulate's. It is billed as "the Original Cajun Restaurant." No other restaurant dares to make that claim in New Orleans (or it would be sued for trademark infringement because Mulate's trademarked that phrase). We ate at Mulate's twice, but the proximity to our hotel wasn't the reason. We went because it is Cajun.

The story of Mulate's is all about a man with a passion for the Cajun culture. He is Kerry Boutte. Boutte is originally from Louisiana. After serving in the military and earning his culinary stripes in the restaurant business, he returned to Louisiana for one purpose: to preserve and promote the Cajun culture.

Cajun isn't just a style of cooking. It is a heritage with a folklore that dates back to those French Canadian exiles from Arcadia who moved to Louisiana in the mid 1700s. For 150 years the Arcadians (Cajuns) lived in relative isolation from the rest of American society. During that time, they developed a distinctive way of life. That's what Kerry Boutte wanted his restaurant to be about—the whole Cajun experience.

So, he's got the food. The appetizers include Cajun boudin balls (spicy pork and rice dressing rolled into balls and deep-fried) and crawfish etouffee (peeled crawfish tails smothered in a stew of chopped peppers, onions, and garlic, and pronounced *A-two-Fay*). For the main course you'll have your choice of seafood with jambalaya. For dessert, we recommend the Atchafalaya mud cake or the bread pudding.

But the food is only part of the Mulate's experience, because it is only part of the Cajun culture. You see, Boutte's restaurant is also a dance hall. And he is as strict about his insistence on authentic Cajun music as he is about the genuine Cajun recipes. So every night of the week includes performances by Cajun bands (with the related styles of rhythm and blues, Creole, zydeco, and swamp pop thrown in).

Kerry Boutte couldn't keep his love for the Cajun culture to himself. He is passionate about sharing it with others. Mulate's offers the tourist a chance to experience the good food, the good music, and the good times of the Cajun culture. It also provides a place where the members of the Cajun community can celebrate their culture with pride and enthusiasm. When you have a chance to experience it, you understand why Boutte is so passionate about sharing it.

MICHAEL: SERVING WITH PASSION

Tourism is the major industry in New Orleans. (It is about the only industry in New Orleans.) And for a city that caters to tourists, you might think that first impressions would be important. Well, that's apparently not the case, at least if your first impression is formed in a cab.

We took quite a few cab rides in New Orleans. And until our last night there, the only good impression from our cab experience was the one made on the rear seat by our rear seats. There is no polite way to say it: Cabs in New Orleans were gritty and smelly. You shouldn't have to worry about getting Slurpee stains on your clothes and contracting a communicable disease just because you want to take a cab ride.

Considering our prior experience, you can imagine how shocked we were on our last night in New Orleans to climb into a cab that was immaculate. The exterior had been washed and waxed. The interior was vacuumed. The windows had been cleaned. And the seats . . . the seats were a treat. There was no danger of stains or sticky residue getting on our clothes. They had been Armor-Alled until the vinyl was supple (which is hard to do in the atmospheric conditions of New Orleans). Our initial inclination upon entering the cab was to give the driver a destination far beyond where we actually wanted to go just so we could spend a little more time in the cab.

We couldn't help asking the driver why his cab was so different from the rest. He didn't hesitate to talk about it; in fact, he enjoyed talking about it: "For me, the kingdom of God is right here in this cab," he said. "This is what God has called me to do. And if he wants me to be a cab driver, then I am going to be the best cab driver there is."

When we reached our destination, we stayed parked at the curb and continued our conversation for about twenty minutes (fortunately the meter was turned off), while the driver explained further his philosophy of serving God by serving others. Here are a few of the things he had to say:

GOD IS WORTHY OF BEING SERVED, AND BECAUSE HE IS THE ALMIGHTY GOD OF THE UNIVERSE, WE SHOULD SERVE HIM WITH ALL OF OUR ENERGIES. WE SHOULD PUT EVERYTHING INTO IT. IN A WORD, WE SHOULD BE PASSIONATE ABOUT IT.

MANY CHRISTIANS THINK ABOUT SERVING GOD ONLY IN GRAND FASHION. THEY PICTURE THEMSELVES ACCOMPLISHING GREAT THINGS. THEY EXPECT THAT THEY'LL GET PASSIONATE ABOUT SERVING GOD WHEN THEY GET TO THE LEVEL OF A BILLY GRAHAM OR A MOTHER TERESA. IN THE MEANTIME,

WHILE THEY HAVE ONLY A MENIAL MINISTRY, THEY DO IT HALFHEARTEDLY.

THE JOB THAT GOD GIVES YOU NOW IS THE ONE HE WANTS YOU TO HAVE. HE MIGHT CALL YOU TO DO SOMETHING DIFFERENT LATER, BUT THAT WILL BE LATER. DON'T SHORTCHANGE GOD NOW.

GOD'S MINISTRIES ALWAYS INVOLVE OTHER PEOPLE. IF YOU LOVE GOD, YOU'LL ACT LOVINGLY TOWARD OTHER PEOPLE.

It was like hearing a sermon in a church service (except nobody passed an offering plate). In fact, it was better than a lot of sermons we have heard. This was one passionate guy—passionate about driving his cab because he was passionate about God. We can honestly say that this cab ride and our conversations with this driver were the most memorable events of our stay in New Orleans.

JESSE: SEARCHING THROUGH PASSION

We met Jesse at the Aquarium of the Americas, which sits right on the Mississippi River. This wasn't a chance meeting like the others, but it definitely wasn't something we could have arranged. We got Jesse's number from a friend and called him out of the blue. We told him we wanted to talk about New Orleans and his take on the meaning of life. Even though we were complete strangers to him, the question energized Jesse. He was anxious to talk with us.

We visited with Alex and Kerry in their restaurants, and Michael shared with us from inside his cab. But Jesse wasn't about to be confined to such conventional spots. The city was his oyster, and he wanted to show us around. We walked up and down the French Quarter, stopping frequently to eat, listen to music, sip a cup of chicory coffee, and indulge in some Key lime pie. All the while Jesse explained his passion and his philosophy of life. We couldn't write fast enough.

Jesse told us that he had moved here less than a year ago to pursue his dream of becoming a professional musician. Things weren't going as he had planned, but his enthusiasm for New Orleans and what he was learning here more than made up for the lack of progress in his career.

"Because I long so much, I think that other people aren't longing enough," Jesse told us. We asked him what he longed for. "Significance. To me significance comes by knowing what you want to relate to others, and by then finding the medium in which to express that." We talked about his medium, which is his guitar and his music. "If just one person relates to what I'm saying through my medium, then I'm happy. When I can encourage others and they respond, I feel significant."

"So you think music can accomplish all of that?" we asked.

"A lot of people see music merely as entertainment, where it provides an escape," he replied. "There's a place for that. But I see music as being able to affect people in a sacred way. Music can provide the intuition and the understanding that gets to the core of who someone is. It can tickle their wings and tug at their spirit. Music can also be a form of grace. It can pull you out of your despair."

Jesse had been thinking a lot about perspective as well. "Perspective is one of the most powerful words in the English language. With a new perspective you can change your whole attitude. My philosophy is, stop worrying and start living in the present. When you live in the past or the future—that's where most people live—you get paralyzed by guilt or by fear.

"When you live in the present, you see the miraculous in the ordinary. We're so used to seeing the mundane in the ordinary. We need to see the miraculous in the ordinary. People have this eternal longing for something beyond themselves." Jesse looked around his adopted city. His eyes were filled with wonder. This young man had thought this stuff through. He spoke with conviction. "They repress it through alcoholism, excess, and pleasure, but they're longing for something more. We need to figure out a way to identify what this longing really is. When we do, then we can help people find true significance and meaning."

THE SOUL OF THE CITY

On our first day in New Orleans, we were completely disgusted. By our last day we were thoroughly charmed. Passion will do that to you, especially if you use your passion as a way to find meaning.

We were packing, ready to leave the Big Easy, when Jesse called us. He had been thinking long and hard about our meeting, and he had one more thing he wanted to tell us. "This is going to sound funny, but I love golf. And the reason is that when you play, you're always in the moment. When you make your golf shot, you can't be thinking about the shot you just shanked, or the next great shot you're going to make. All that matters is the shot you're taking right now. That's why you practice. That's why you play. For the moment."

"Gee, thanks, Jesse," we said. "We'll remember that next time we hit the links." (Truth is, neither of us play golf.)

"No, hear me out. This isn't about golf; it's about the moment. When you get in the moment, you get in the zone. That's why I like music, especially jazz. When everybody in a group clicks together, they click in the moment. They're in the zone."

It was starting to make sense. Golf, jazz, life. Three things that take a lifetime to master, and in each case they unfold moment by moment. "To me, life is a constant rehearsal for the moment," Jesse concluded.

As we drove out of town, it hit us. Maybe the meaning of life isn't something you work up to, and then all of the sudden you have it in one big chunk. Perhaps meaning is found in little moments lived in the here and now. Jesse would agree with that. For him living in the present is the only way to open the doors to the future. After all, isn't that where we will find that something beyond ourselves that gives us ultimate meaning?

departure
03214

NEXT STOP: DALLAS

6

arrival mileage

0 3 7 7 1

DALLAS:

Winning the Game of Life

We are the first to admit that our search for the meaning of life was a limited one. Even though we personally talked to more than a thousand people in the course of our fourteen-week, ten-thousand-mile journey, we barely scratched the surface of this deep subject. First of all, we restricted our search to the United States, which has only 5 percent of the planet's 6 billion people. We then narrowed the beam even more by focusing on the cities, and only eleven of them at that.

America's heart may be off the highways in the smaller towns, but its soul is in the cities. The difference is this: The heart is traditionally the seat of emotion. You love with your heart, your heart can ache, and it can even break. By contrast, the soul is the place of discovery. Before a big decision, you do some soul-searching. Longing comes from the depths of your soul, and so does the search for meaning. If the heart feels, then the soul thinks. The heart responds; the soul discovers.

Once we knew we had to visit America's cities in order to get the answer to our question, we had to decide which cities to visit. This wasn't as difficult as it might seem. All cities have personalities, some kind of distinction that sets them apart. Distinctiveness was part of the criteria used to select each of the eleven cities. Gertrude Stein once said of Oakland, California: "There's no there there." We wanted to visit cities where there was a "there."

DALLAS IS MORE THAN FOOTBALL

Which brings us to Dallas. How did Dallas make the *Bruce & Stan Search for the Meaning of Life* cut, but not Houston or St. Louis? Look at it this way:

There has never been a television show named *Houston*. Despite their success, the St. Louis Rams are not "America's Team." (They haven't even been in St. Louis for very long.) And when you think of big business and big deals and bigger-than-life issues in a big state, you don't think of Albuquerque. You think of Dallas.

We knew there was a "there" in Dallas—a soul that defines it—and we knew it would lead us to the meaning of life Texas style. We just weren't sure what it was. As we drove into Dallas from the east, we thought about the three things people normally associate with Dallas:

- The assassination of JFK
- J. R. Ewing and the television show *Dallas*
- The Dallas Cowboys

We immediately threw out the first two items on that list. We weren't going to find any meaning there. (And besides, our guess is that *Dallas* reruns are popular only in Riyadh, Saudi Arabia, and that's only because they love stories about oil.)

That left the Dallas Cowboys, or more precisely, football. Like basketball is to Indiana, football is to Texas—a religion. Surely we would find people in Dallas willing to talk about football and the meaning of life. So we drove around Dallas looking for clues.

What we found is that it isn't just football that defines Dallas (at least not since the Landry era). We were impressed with the great emphasis on professional sports of all kinds. We first spotted Reunion Arena, home of the Dallas Mavericks basketball team and the Dallas Stars hockey team, right off the freeway. (In fact, you have to circle around it to get into the downtown area.) If you are taking the often-traveled I-30 to neighboring Fort Worth, you drive by the majestic Ballpark in Arlington, home of the Texas Rangers. If you are going into or leaving Dallas via the DFW airport, you can't miss driving by Texas Stadium, where the Dallas Cowboys play. (The home of the Cowboys is actually in the suburb of Irving, but the "Irving Cowboys" sounds more like a team owned by a guy from Schenectady, so that was never an option.)

So Dallas is really about sports, not just football. Yet is it sports alone that gives people meaning, or is it deeper than that? All sports are based on the spirit of competition and the drive to succeed. Is that where we would find the answers to our question?

Since we didn't have a list of professional athletes in our Rolodex, we decided to set our sights on a more realistic target. We drove north of Dallas to the suburb of Plano, where the spirit of competition in all areas of life—sports, business, and just plain living—is fierce. Several international corporations are headquartered here, and hundreds of smaller but no less successful companies—all fighting for market share in their respective fields—dot the grassy landscape.

No Longer America's Team

A curious thing happened in 1989 when a new owner bought the Dallas Cowboys and promptly fired Coach Tom Landry. Landry had been the only coach since the team was formed in 1960. After some disastrous seasons, Landry and a changing cast of players amassed a string of twenty straight winning seasons, including thirteen division titles and two Super Bowl championships. With his trademark fedora and stone-faced demeanor, Landry was the definition of class and integrity. Under his rock-solid leadership, the Cowboys became "America's Team." All that changed in the years after Landry left. Oh, the Cowboys continued to win; in fact they've won three Super Bowls since. But things have changed, and America knows it. People will always admire a winner, but they embrace a winner who keeps the game in perspective. That's what Landry did, and that's why people everywhere loved his Cowboys. Now, like so many teams in sports at all levels, the Cowboys have made winning their only goal at whatever the cost. It's hard to keep your perspective when that happens.

NEVER LET THEM SEE YOU SWEAT

We found a family that truly typifies the spirit of Plano and Dallas. Ken Johnson is a senior executive in an international manufacturing company. His wife, Jeanie, is a medical professional. Ken and Jeanie's two sons know all about the competitive Plano school system. It was 110 degrees in Plano the day we met three of the four Johnsons, and we were relieved when they invited us into their home. We envisioned a cool afternoon sipping Texas sweet tea in their parlor (that's what you call living rooms in this part of the country) as we discussed the meaning of life with this very nice family. But it wasn't to be. Ken decided that he and his older son, Erik, needed to jump in our car and give us a tour of Plano in order to get an "accurate sense of the place." We protested mildly, explaining to Ken that the air conditioning in our rental car wasn't working properly. We even cited various accounts of people in Texas dying from heat exhaustion in ovenlike vehicles, but Ken insisted. "We'll just keep the windows rolled down so the air flows through," he said. We could hardly wait.

Dallas CityFacts

Dallas

FOUNDED: 1841
POPULATION: 1,075,894
METRO AREA: 2,676,000
DFW METROPLEX: Over 4 million
NICKNAME: Big D
BUT WE CALL IT: Dallas "Thank the Lord for Air Conditioning" Texas
KNOWN FOR: Oil, cowboys, and a presidential assassination
FAMOUS NATIVES: Trini Lopez, Aaron Spelling, Stephen Stills, Sharon Tate, Lee Trevino

Actually, our car tour of Plano was amazingly insightful. Erik directed us to Plano Senior High School, his alma mater of two months. This school of thirty-five hundred has only two grades—eleventh and twelfth—but it is a sports powerhouse. Erik showed us the gym, where we saw huge banners proclaiming PSHS as state champions in several sports, and we drove to the thirty-thousand-seat football stadium. "Season tickets sell out months before the season starts," Erik said. We were dumbfounded. "So you're saying that high school football is pretty important here?"

Ken explained that there is incredible pressure to win at this level. "Football games in this stadium are the major social outings of the week for thousands of Plano families. The only problem is that when the team doesn't win as much, the enthusiasm wanes. Just like everywhere else, people love a winner."

We looked at Erik, a good-looking kid with a great attitude. "So how do you keep everything in perspective?" we asked him. "How do you keep from being consumed by winning, especially when the whole town is depending on it?"

"I want you to meet someone," Erik replied.

TUESDAYS, THURSDAYS, AND SUNDAYS WITH TOM

We were surprised when we met Erik's friend. He wasn't a high school buddy with a cool car. Tom Hunt was a man in his mid thirties with a wife and three daughters. (No, Erik wasn't friends with Tom because of his daughters, even though they were very cute.) Tom is your average, good-looking ex-jock with a winning smile and a nice house—with one difference. He has a full weight room in his garage, and it's not just to flex his own muscles. Every Tuesday, Thursday, and Sunday evening Tom and a half dozen young men lift weights together and talk about what really matters in life.

"I enjoy working with men my own age," Tom said, "but I realized that I needed to reach guys at a younger age before they get stuck in their ways." So Tom decided to combine his passion for mentoring with his passion for lifting weights. He put the word out that his garage would be open three times a week for guys to come lift for an hour or so. Tom would instruct them, lift with them, and then afterward they would "cool down" and talk. It wasn't long before the guys came and lifted and talked. And it wasn't long after that that their discussions turned to serious matters, like life and relationships and God.

That's where Erik came in. He met Tom through his dad, and within a short time the two formed a special bond. "Erik has taught me to relate to high school kids in a way that's out of the box," Tom explained. And for his part, Erik has learned what it means to be in a dynamic relationship where you learn from a mentor as you teach someone younger. He told us, "I feel a responsibility to these younger guys, because they won't always relate to Tom. And someday they are going to become mentors to others."

We were feeling pretty warm inside as we left Tom's garage/gym, and it wasn't because our car's interior had heated to 180 degrees. We were so impressed with the maturity and dedication of the people we had just met. For them, winning the game of life was more important than winning the game. They were no less competitive in sports and business than the next guy, but they kept everything in perspective. We headed back to Dallas wondering if we would find any more people like these.

CONFESSIONS OF A LITTLE LEAGUE DAD

Everyone knows the stereotype of the Little League father who acts like a raving lunatic in the stands, the kind who annoys everyone around him and embarrasses his own kid with tirades and emotional outbursts. Of course, not all dads are like that, but apparently the Dallas Little League is thinking of instituting some kind of twelve-step program for the overcompetitive, emotionally charged, testosterone-enhanced rageaholics.

Is T-ball Worth Dying For?

The people we interviewed in Dallas said that competitive instincts and the obsession with winning start early in life. We were thinking that they meant the high school level. They laughed and said that it starts at least ten years before that, when a four-year-old takes his or her first swing at a T-ball.

We didn't like what we heard when they explained Texas T-ball to us. It sounded like New Age Baseball. And worse than that, it sounded socialistic. So un-American (or at least so un-Dallas). Think about it:

- They don't keep track of outs. Everybody gets a turn to hit.
- They don't keep track of how many runs are scored.
- There is no winner or loser.

The concept is all about skill development and building self-esteem, so no child is supposed to walk off the field feeling like a loser; that means all of them are winners. Or at least that is the way it is supposed to be.

But it isn't. Those little Texas tykes are savvy enough to know about real life. They apparently keep track of the score (even though they aren't supposed to). And their parents do too. So when the game is over, one group is taunting the others (and those are the parents).

It seems that the ugly (and often violent) side of athletic competition gets worse as the kids and parents get older. But Dallas isn't the only place this happens. During the time we were driving across the country, the desire to win cost a man his life. Michael Costin, a young father of three boys, was the volunteer coach of kids' hockey team. Another father, Thomas Junta, didn't like the way Coach Costin was handling the team. The men got into a fight, and Junta allegedly beat Costin until he was brain dead. Junta was charged with manslaughter.

We met up with one of these dads when we returned to Dallas, and it gave us another angle on this whole business of competition and winning. He admitted to being in a "recovery" process, having made the transition from being from a "bad Little League dad" to a "good Little League dad." We asked if we could interview him about how sports had become so important to him that it threw his life out of balance. He consented to our request, and the next day he revealed his shame to us in a soundproof room (not because he was worried about preserving his anonymity, but because he worked at a radio recording studio).

The story you are about to read is his. Any similarity to actual events or real people is intentional, because it is all true.

Call me Chuck X, and heed me well. I used to be considered a gentle husband, a loving father, and a respected businessman. But wait! My story really starts way before this.

I guess it all began when I was in high school. I was the star of the baseball team. I was popular back then, so popular that I could do whatever I wanted and nobody messed with me. Everybody cheered for me on and off the field.

I played on the baseball team in college too. Only I wasn't as good. Not as many people paid attention to me. Fewer people laughed at my antics and told me I was great. I could have been drafted into the big leagues if only the coach had played me more.

I married my high school sweetheart. I made her wear my high school lettermen's jacket at our wedding reception. We both wanted to have kids right away. She was anxious to be a mom; I was anxious to be a coach.

We had a boy (thanks to my virile XY chromosomes). I promised my wife I wouldn't get all psycho about the sports thing until our son was old enough. I waited and waited and waited. Finally he turned four and I enrolled him in T-ball. (Fortunately I had been working with him on hitting and fielding drills since he was two, whenever his mom went to her evening aerobics class.)

It was T-ball, then peewee league, and then on to Little League. I was the coach for my son's team at every level. I really emphasized team spirit. It was all for one, and I was the one. But some of the parents didn't see it that way. They complained when I swore at their kids for not hustling—

hey, it was just a motivational technique. And then even my own son started slacking off. He wanted to quit, but I wouldn't let him. I knew that deep down he really wanted to be the major leaguer that I could never be. The more the kids dogged it, the more intense I became.

Then there was a mutiny. The other parents kicked me out as coach. Even my own wife voted against me. They made me sit in the bleachers—with the women and the men who never strapped on a jock. It was humiliating. But I didn't let it dampen my enthusiasm. I was still supporting the team by yelling at our players, cursing the umpire, and taunting the opponents with crude remarks.

Before long, I was banned from the bleachers. They stripped me of my team cap. They wouldn't let me near the dugouts or the other parents. I had to sit in a lawn chair by myself fifty yards past the right-field fence. I wasn't allowed to speak, just wave a Dallas Dynamo's Little League pennant. And my wife said that I couldn't talk baseball to my son at home, or she'd take my pennant away.

After two years of good behavior in this mandatory exile, they gave me a job. I get to scrape the gum off the underneath side of the bleachers after every game. If I continue to control my temper, then next year I can sell wieners at the concession stand.

Well, that's my story. I'm not really involved with baseball anymore, but at least my son is talking to me again. (And his batting average is a lot higher than it used to be.) Maybe others can learn from my story before it is too late for them. So for any dads who might follow in my footsteps, let me just say, "A little cheering isn't a problem, but if you start sharpening you kid's cleats, then watch out."

OK, so maybe he didn't say all of that exactly, but almost. Chuck (his real name) had gotten out of control. But he had a few guys who "were good enough friends and strong enough people" to take him aside and tell him the damage he was doing to himself, his son, and the rest of the team. After this confrontation, Chuck went to his son and asked, "Is this what is really happening?" His son had the guts to say, "Yes it is." Then the two of them got into a conversation about how Chuck needed to change. Chuck has come through that experience with a changed perspective, and he gave us some helpful insights about how sports and competition impact the meaning of life for many people. He explained it in terms of being a "bad Little League dad" versus being a "good Little League dad."

A BAD LITTLE LEAGUE DAD: IT'S ALL ABOUT ME

According to Chuck, some parents are completely self-centered.

They are living out their failed, miserable lives through their kids. They want to make sure that their child achieves the success that they weren't good enough to achieve for themselves.

Their entire emotional state is geared to how well their child is playing. If the kid excels on the field, then the parents are congratulated in the stands. The parents want the attention and accolades that come from their child's performance. But if the kid has a bad game, then the parents go home miserable.

A GOOD LITTLE LEAGUE DAD: IT'S ALL ABOUT LIFE

In contrast, other parents have a balanced approach and use sports as a metaphor for life.

They recognize that participation in sports is an opportunity to prepare their children to become better adults. If the kids can learn to handle themselves on the field, they'll be better equipped to handle situations off the field.

They use sports as a way to teach their children the importance of team-work. This is an important concept to learn because it is useful in families, at school, and in the working world.

They use defeats and discouragement to teach their children that disap-pointment is a part of life. They emphasize that an important part of life is learning how to handle the disappointment, whether it comes from going 0-for-3 at age fifteen, or not getting the raise at work when you are thirty-five.

And they use sports to teach their child that there is nothing wrong with winning, but it must be done with class and graciousness.

We complimented Chuck at his obvious transformation and his astute observations. He assured us that he was in a process, and that it was still a struggle to maintain his composure and keep the proper focus. (His wife still brings a lawn chair to every game just in case he needs to sit by himself fifty yards past the right-field fence.)

IS THERE LIFE AFTER THE GAME?

Like every other male who is more likely to be mistaken for the Michelin Man than an Ironman, we have a hard time relating to the professional athlete. We wondered if there are any downsides to being paid ridiculous amounts of money to play a game better than most other people. About the only one we could come up with was: Life is over when you retire from the game.

We know the superstars can parlay their celebrity status into different business ventures. (Car dealerships and restaurants seem to be the post-playing business ventures of choice.) But what about all of the professional players who never get famous enough to get a network announcing job or a cushy business PR position when they retire? How do they feel about the prospects for life after they're through playing the game they love? And what about the multitudes of professional players in the farm clubs, minor leagues, and semipro ranks who at some point have to finally hang it up without ever reaching their dream of making it to the "Bigs"? Their entire lives have been spent focused on their sport, and now what?

Billy Allen gave us some answers to these questions. He was the perfect guy to interview about these questions because his life fit the profile perfectly.

Billy's dad is Sonny Allen, who has coached basketball for forty years. Sonny was the highly successful basketball coach at SMU for many years, he coached the Dallas Mavericks in the NBA, and he came out of retirement to coach the Sacramento Monarchs of the WNBA.

As you can imagine, it was expected that Billy would be a basketball player even before he was born. And he was a basketball star in high school and at SMU. He set an NCAA record for career assists in 1983. Everything looked bright for Billy when the Dallas Mavericks drafted him. But he didn't make the cut at training camp!

It was at this point that Billy's dream of playing in the NBA started to deteriorate. He didn't let go of it right away, but it kept crumbling:

- He tried out and was cut from three different NBA teams.
- He played two seasons with the Sarasota Stingers of the Canadian Basketball Association.
- Then he tried his hand at coaching. He became an assistant coach for his dad, but his dad was fired at the end of the season.

Here was a guy who had devoted a quarter of a century to basketball. He ate it and he breathed it, and then it came to screeching halt. Basketball was the meaning in his life, and then it was over. We wanted to know where he finds his meaning in life now.

Billy's postbasketball life wasn't in shambles and ruin. In fact, he has been quite successful as an executive for an athletic shoe manufacturer. Nonetheless, for about five or six years after leaving the hardwood, he didn't have anything to do with basketball. With a great marriage and family and a good job, Billy found his meaning elsewhere. But what about the first twenty-five years of his life? Was it all just a waste? Would he have been better off skipping basketball and channeling all his efforts during those years into something else? Billy told us a story that more than answered our questions.

In 1993, Billy was sitting with his wife at Legacy Drive Baptist Church. (In Dallas, there are so many Baptist churches that they have run out of names. The new ones have to be named after streets.) The pastor challenged people to use their talents for God. He said that God gives everyone special abilities, and we need to find ways to use those skills in service to God. Billy's wife jabbed him in the ribs as the pastor spoke.

Billy and his wife approached the pastor after the service. "I'd be glad to help," Billy said as he rubbed his injured ribs, "but all I know about is basketball." The pastor laughed and told them that the church had been trying for many years to start a youth basketball clinic but had never found the person with the athletic knowledge and management skills to get it going.

As they say, the rest is history. For more than five years Billy has been the commissioner of the Legacy Drive Skills and Drills Basketball Camp. There are sessions during spring break and in the fall. Billy gets to coach young kids and teach them shooting and ball-handling skills. He and the other coaches teach them the basics of basketball, but that's not all. Each kid is given a Bible and taught principles that translate into being a good team player. No one makes any money off of this basketball camp. (The enrollment fee covers the

> "[Success] is not about winning or losing . . . the issue is a lot bigger than that.
> It has to do with what God wants to accomplish on this earth and how he can best achieve that goal."
> —*Kurt Warner*

costs of the balls, jerseys, and Bibles that are given to each kid, and there are people in the church who give scholarships for the kids who can't afford to pay.) Billy does it out of his love for God . . . and his love of the game.

The basketball camps actually helped Billy put his life into perspective. Now he doesn't view those first twenty-five years of his life as ending in failure or as a waste of time. He sees meaning and purpose in those basketball years—God's purpose. "When you get cut from a team, you have to realize that there is other meaning out there," he told us. For Billy Allen, the meaning of life involves basketball, but not for the sake of the game. He uses basketball as a means to impact the lives of other people and help them find meaning for their own lives.

GOD IS BIGGER THAN THE GAME

Billy Allen's story encouraged us because it shows that you can find meaning even if your lifelong ambition is not realized. (That was good news for us since we have resigned ourselves to the fact that an Olympic gold medal won't be hanging on our walls. Imagine, training all those years with the hacky sack, only to learn that it isn't an Olympic event.) But we still wanted to know: Can you find meaning in your life by winning it all?

We don't know any famous athletes, past or present, but we know people who know people who do. So, as we did so often on our trip, we made a few calls using the six-degrees-of-separation theory. (Sometimes people made the connection between us and their cousin's friend's nephew, but more often we got these people so confused that they thought they must know us or be related to us.) We pulled this scam on former PGA tournament champion Rik Massengale, and it worked.

Rik was on the PGA tour from 1970 to 1982. He won three tournaments and was a recognizable figure on the tour, competing toe to toe (or should we say, golf club to golf club) with the likes of Tom Watson and Jack Nicklaus. We figured that life must have been sweet and easy for Rik then, but that's not the story he told. He emphasized the emptiness and insecurity of it all:

IT IS HARD TO KEEP A POSITIVE ATTITUDE AS A GOLFER.
THERE IS SOMETHING ABOUT EACH HOLE THAT DISAPPOINTS YOU.

GOLF INTENSIFIES AND ACCELERATES LIFE. A GUY IN AN OFFICE WOULD HAVE TO WORK FOR AN ENTIRE MONTH TO EXPERIENCE ALL OF THE EMOTIONS AND TRIALS THAT ARE EXPERIENCED BY A PROFESSIONAL GOLFER IN EIGHTEEN HOLES.

Rik was at the top of his game in 1974, but his life off the fairways was falling apart. His marriage was suffering, and he couldn't make sense of his life. This turmoil eventually started to affect his play. With no other options, Rik went to hear an evangelist who spoke at a Pro-Am tournament. You may recognize his name: Billy Graham.

Up until that point, golf was Rik's god. But Rik moved golf out of the center of his life and made Jesus Christ what he was living for. It was this decision that turned Rik's life around.

Notice that we didn't say that making Christ the focal point of his life turned Rik's golf game around. (Actually it did. He went on to win tournaments in 1974, 1975, and 1976.) But Rik doesn't view God as a rabbit's foot that hangs from his golf bag to bring good luck. The tournament victories are only incidental aspects of his faith. The real benefit was a change in the focus of his life.

> "And how do you benefit if you gain the whole world but lose your own soul in the process?"
> —Mark 8:36

"If you don't know Jesus Christ, then success is your only hope. It takes constant winning to make you happy and keep the respect of your peers. And once you start losing, you can get under the pile real quick. But if you know Christ, you have a different perspective and priority regarding success."

That change of perspective is something that Rik is trying to pass on to younger golfers. Rik is currently the president of College Golf Fellowship, an organization that works with NCAA golf teams, teaching them principles about life from an eternal perspective. He can get the attention of these college golfers because they know he speaks from personal experience.

"I tell them that if they base their happiness on how they play golf, then they aren't going to be very happy people. Golf is an emotional roller coaster. It changes day to day. Heck, it changes hole to hole. And they know that.

"I try to tell them that Christ can give them fulfillment and peace and joy in the midst of all the hassles they have in golf. I tell them that a relationship with Christ can give them a real purpose for living. I encourage them to keep competing and pursuing their golf; but I also tell them not to neglect the spiritual dimension of their life."

Rik didn't hesitate when we asked him about the meaning of life. "Significance in life comes when you can use the gifts and talents God has given you to further his kingdom. True significance and fulfillment come by sharing God with others and helping them grow in a relationship with him."

MOVING FROM SUCCESS TO SIGNIFICANCE

There are fifty million people in the U.S. who play golf. But 90 percent of them can't break 90. That means there is a lot of frustration out on the fairways and greens. What an opportunity for a golf psychologist—if there was such a thing. Actually, there is, and we found him.

Dr. David Cook is the president of Mental Advantage, Inc., a performance enhancement firm that consults in both the sports and business arenas. Before starting this company, David served for twelve years as the director of Applied Sport and Performance Psychology at the University of Kansas, where he counseled over fifteen hundred athletes and coaches. He is a past president of the National Sport Psychology Academy. Dr. Cook's clients include one hundred professional golfers; elite players and teams from the National Basketball Association, the National Football League, and Major League Baseball; as well as executives from companies like Compaq, American Express, Texas Instruments, and Bayer Corp.

We caught up with Dr. Cook at his other job—on the driving range at WaterChase Golf Academy in Fort Worth. (Any guy who can finagle his career so his office is on the golf course is our hero. This excludes, of course, the guy in that little cart covered with chicken wire who gets pelted as he traverses the driving range scooping up the golf balls.) Dr. Cook is also the director of the Mindset Academy at WaterChase, a new state-of-the-art facility where he teaches the mental aspects of golf. There is no other place like it in the country.

Since we wanted to know how winning and success figured into the meaning of life, Dr. Cook was our go-to guy. We were a little intimidated before we met him. He has gotten into the minds of so many world-class athletes, we thought he might see us and immediately recognize that our brains are in a state of severe atrophy. But our fears were dispelled when we met him. (Meeting a world-famous psychologist isn't very intimidating when he stands there in a golf shirt and offers to buy you a Gatorade at the clubhouse.)

We spoke with Dave on a variety of topics, but all of them related to the meaning of life in one way or another. Our Q & A session went something like this:

B & S: What in the heck is Sports Psychology?

Dr. Dave: I'll explain it simply because I know that is the only way you two guys will understand it. (We knew it! He could see into our brains!) Sports psychology is taking the engineering aspects of the physical side of sports and combining them with the logical and mental parts of the game. I teach people how to be effective in the way they use the brains God gave them. It is combining the mechanics of the sport with the mental aspects.

B & S: Your entire career is about helping people become winners. The benefits of winning seem obvious, but is there a negative side to it?

Dr. Dave: Definitely. I have spoken with many players and coaches in all sports who have won tournaments and championships. Shortly after the celebration is over, they say the victory hasn't been all that fulfilling. They worked so hard and so long for it, but when it came, it didn't bring them the ultimate satisfaction that they were hoping for. Quite often they say, "But maybe it just takes winning two in a row. Maybe it will be worth it when we repeat."

B & S: So does the next victory lead to fulfillment?

Dr. Dave: Not at all. The game, whether it is sports or business, is not really about victory. It becomes a continual chase for an elusive sense of fulfillment. People believe they will find it if they keep going higher and getting better. But the higher they go, the smaller their world becomes. Their contacts with the outside world shrink around them, and there is increasing futility. For them, personal success is measured by the terms of their new contracts. Status within your peer group is relative to your contract figures.

B & S: You've painted a bleak picture of being a superstar athlete. But is this the case for everyone?

Dr. Dave: There are many athletes who find fulfillment in their lives. They are the ones who have kept their worlds from closing in on them. It's all about perspective. Let's take a guy on the PGA Tour. If he knows and appreciates the facts that (a) God loves him, (b) his wife loves him, and (c) his kids love him, then he is going to say, "How important can this twelve-foot putt be?"

B & S: You make it sound like a God-fearing family man has lost his competitive edge?

Dr. Dave: Remember, it's all about perspective. Here's the strategy that I teach: Your security in life is directly related to your priorities. If your whole life and self-worth are wrapped up in golf—if it all boils down to one shot—then you don't have the freedom to perform. But if you know that you have significance outside of golf, if you have other and greater priorities in your life, then you have complete freedom to compete. God can be that greater priority in your life.

B & S: You keep bringing God into the mix. Can that be an athlete's secret weapon?

Dr. Dave: God doesn't have favorite teams he cheers for. And sports is not about theology. But spiritual faith can be a very important component in maintaining the focus on your goal. It brings that broader perspective that I was talking about. The athletes and business executives who have a balanced perspective are those who have:

- A sense of purpose: They know why they are doing it.
- A sense of accountability: They are responsible to someone else; it's not just all about them.
- A sense of nobility: Their efforts have a value that is bigger than what they do.
- A sense of reward: Knowing that what you do benefits yourself and other.

These factors are all part of a strong spiritual faith.

B & S: Can you give us any real-life examples from athletes that you have counseled? We'll keep what you tell us confidential. We promise not to put it in a book or anything.

Dr. Dave: I'll give you two. The first one is David Robinson, the star center for the San Antonio Spurs. I was working with Robinson in 1998 and '99 when the Spurs won the NBA Championship and he was the league's MVP. Robinson is an outspoken Christian, and I asked how all of those accolades affected him. It was interesting to me that he didn't talk about these things in the context of personal success. Instead, he considered them significant because they gave him more opportunities to share his faith. He is definitely a fierce competitor, but his life is about much more than just basketball. He wants to share that message with other people. The championship and MVP honors give him more opportunity to do that. He has made the mental transition in his game from success to significance. That's the sense of purpose, accountability, nobility, and reward all rolled into one guy. One very tall guy.

B & S: Who is the other example?

Dr. Dave: That would be me. I resigned my position as director of Applied Sport and Performance Psychology at the University of Kansas because my job wasn't giving me a sense of real value. There didn't appear to be much ultimate meaning in helping athletes perform better just so they could get a higher salary. Then I started to see my profession from an eternal perspective. What I do isn't about religion, although many effective techniques are built on scriptural principles. But it is about helping people come to grips with what is important in life. It is helping them assess their own priorities and perspective.

Our interview with Dave Cook came to an end just as we finished off the last drop of Gatorade. Our heads were swirling with what he had told us. He was a guy dealing with meaning-of-life issues on a grand scale. And it wasn't just a theory to him. He had that sense of purpose, accountability, nobility, and reward in his own life. We knew it when we asked him to give us his own personal meaning-of-life statement, and he said: "To pull people from the ashes of the bonfire of insignificance."

THE SOUL OF THE CITY

We were excited to leave Dallas for three reasons. First, we were heading north, where the weather was definitely cooler. Second, we were officially more than halfway done with our search for the meaning of life. Third, our search had taken on a new twist. For the first time in our journey, every person we interviewed talked about the same stuff. It was as if Ken, Erik, Tom, Chuck, Billy, Rik, and Dave had met before we arrived and decided to give us the same ideas. But with the exception of Ken, Erik, and Tom, these guys didn't know each other. They weren't in the same professions, and they didn't even play the same sports. Yet the principles they lived by and their conclusions about the meaning of life were strangely consistent.

Young Erik the student talked about keeping things in perspective, and so did Dr. Dave the sports psychologist. Tom, Chuck, and Billy were using three different sports to teach the same life principles, and they found tremendous fulfillment in the process. Rik and Dave believed that true success comes when your life has a strong spiritual faith. Dave's image of pulling people from the "bonfire of insignificance" was burned in our collective memory. Could there be any higher calling in life?

A few years ago we had the privilege of meeting with Bob Briner, an amazing man who built a hugely successful sports-marketing company in Dallas. He became a hero to many young athletes, and eventually to thousands of young artists and musicians as well. Like the people we met with in Dallas, Bob used sports and business as a platform to share his faith in Christ with others.

Bob graciously agreed to meet with us because we were interested in being better communicators. He gave us some very practical advice, which we use to this day. More important, he challenged us to be out in the culture as salt and light. Bob knew that sports was the perfect vehicle for Christians to live out their faith, and he pointed out that sports at all levels have a significant spiritual influence. In other words, the world of sports is already pretty salty.

"By contrast," Bob Briner wrote, "the culture-shaping professions are especially salt-free." He was referring to the media, the arts, literature, and academics. "This is where we need to be." Bob wasn't saying—and neither are we—that you shouldn't use sports as a platform for sharing the meaning you have found in your life. The message is this: Don't think you have to be a superior athlete or a national champion before people will listen to you. In fact, you don't have to be at the top of your game in any profession in order to have an impact on others. "We do not have to be the best to be effective, but we do have to be at our best" (*Roaring Lambs,* Zondervan).

departure
0 4 1 3 4

NEXT STOP: CHICAGO

7

CHICAGO:
Spirituality for This Life and the Next

There is a considerable distance between Dallas and Chicago. And it's a lot more than just the 928 miles that separate the two cities. The cultural differences are just as great as the geographical divide. In Dallas, the pace of life is comfortably slow. Maybe it's the heat that retards body metabolism. Perhaps it's the fact that the Dallas/Fort Worth metroplex is so doggone big (to use Texas terminology) that everything is spread out and you can't get anywhere in a hurry. Maybe the legendary Texas drawl—which automatically adds an extra syllable to any word you say, so that even simple conversations seem to take an eternity—is to blame.

Not so with Chicago. It has a hustle about it. There is intensity in this city. But its unique personality is unlike the East Coast cities we visited. New York was intense, to be sure, but there the people seemed uptight. In Chicago, people are intense because they work hard; but they also play hard. This is a fun town because its citizens like to have a good time.

Chicago doesn't get the attention it deserves as a major city. It's the biggest city in the Midwest, but only third in the nation. While Chicago sits on a large body of water, it isn't on either coast, where New York and Los Angeles—numbers one and two—rake in all the attention. Chicago isn't a sexy city like the Big Apple or Lala Land. There's no Times Square or Hollywood, no glitz and glamour that create an aura of fantasy. This is a working town. New York may supply the culture and Los Angeles the entertainment, but Chicago brings home the bacon. (This is literally true. Hog futures are an important part of the Chicago Board of Trade.)

Somehow we don't think the residents of Chicago mind being number three. They know that Chicago represents the best of what Middle America is all about.

RESIDENTIAL RESURGENCE

According to the U.S. Census, more than 31,000 building permits for residential construction have been issued in the Chicago area in each of the past five years. That is more than any other American city except Atlanta and Phoenix. The residential building boom in most U.S. cities is due to an increase in population (such as the gain of 600,000 in the Atlanta metropolitan area in the 1990s). But the population of the city of Chicago increased by only 25,000 in the last decade. So, the residential resurrection in Chicago is from people choosing to live in the downtown area rather than the suburbs. In fact, many of these new urban dwellers are suburban empty nesters who fled the city in past decades. Others are members of the younger, digital demographic who desire the vitality of the urban environment, which Chicago offers in great measure.

WHAT'S GOING UP DOWNTOWN

When you think of skyscrapers—those majestic monoliths of concrete, steel, and glass that soar heavenward—you automatically think of New York. You shouldn't. The world's first skyscraper, the ten-story Home Insurance Building, was constructed in Chicago in 1885. The Sears Tower, America's tallest building, is located in Chicago.

But there is more to downtown Chicago than those two potential answers for *Who Wants to Be a Millionaire*. Chicago is in the midst of a business-building boom. Almost nine thousand commercial building permits were issued by the city last year. We saw the largest office building under construction in the nation—all thirty-seven stories and 1.8 million square feet of it—on Dearborn Avenue.

SHOPPING

There are two reasons we are totally disinterested in shopping, especially if you are talking about the trendy boutiques on Rodeo Drive in Beverly Hills or the exotic designer shops on Fifth Avenue in New York. First, we are guys, so we aren't really interested in shopping for something you can't wear to work or plug into a wall socket. Secondly, we are practical, so if it's going to cost as much as a new car, we would be much more comfortable shopping in a dealership showroom. But we'll make an exception for Chicago, because this is a city where we can shop.

Stan, who is more fashion conscious, was interested in the enormous Nordstrom department store recently built on Michigan Avenue, Chicago's most prestigious shopping street (otherwise known as the "Miracle Mile," because it's a miracle if you can get away from Michigan Avenue without spending anything). Bruce is more of a hardware guy. He was delighted to see that Sears is returning to the core of the city with a new store on State Street (just a few blocks from its former flagship store that was abandoned in the 1980s). So, whether you want a cashmere sweater or a chrome-plated socket set, Chicago sells what most Americans want to buy.

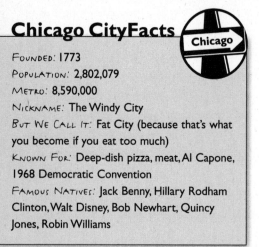

Chicago CityFacts

FOUNDED: 1773
POPULATION: 2,802,079
METRO: 8,590,000
NICKNAME: The Windy City
BUT WE CALL IT: Fat City (because that's what you become if you eat too much)
KNOWN FOR: Deep-dish pizza, meat, Al Capone, 1968 Democratic Convention
FAMOUS NATIVES: Jack Benny, Hillary Rodham Clinton, Walt Disney, Bob Newhart, Quincy Jones, Robin Williams

FOOD

Many American cities are identified with a certain type of food. Boston has its clam chowder and cream pie, Philadelphia has the cheese steak sandwich, and Denver has its omelet. In Chicago, one of the basic food groups is pizza. Not just any type of pizza, but Chicago-style, deep-dish pizza—the kind so heavy you can't lift it to your mouth without outside help. We learned that the preferred position for consumption of this local dietary mainstay is to lower your head to table level and slide the massive slice directly into your eating orifice.

OPTIMISM

Chicago is the city that best exemplifies the optimistic spirit of America. Boston might be aloof, and New York might be cynical, but Chicago is incredibly positive. How else do you explain the fan loyalty enjoyed by the Chicago Cubs, America's perennial losers? It's not that Chicagoans don't know how to win. The Bulls and the Bears (Chicago, not Wall Street) have won several championships. Other cities might reject a baseball team that hasn't won a World Series since Theodore Roosevelt was president, but not Chicago. There is a sense of family in this city. They want the best for each other, and they'll keep hoping for the best until it comes. ("Wait until next year" is such a positive slogan, don't you think?)

OUR KIND OF TOWN

Both of us love Chicago. We've been here many times as a writing team to tape interviews or appear live on one of several national radio and television networks located here. (These aren't big-league networks like you have in New York and Los Angeles. These are grassroots, middle America, Bruce & Stan kind of media.)

Both of us can trace our roots to Chicago as well. Bruce was born in the blue-collar suburb of Berwyn, and Stan spent the first few years of his life in the eastern suburb of Wheaton, where his father was a ministerial student at the college there.

As familiar as we were with Chicago, we must honestly tell you that we had never before thought about Chicago's defining character. Even after our steak dinner at Gibson's, where the rib eye is so tender you can cut it with a fork, we weren't sure of Chicago's true identity. We thought we had it in the middle of a deep-dish monstrosity at Pizzeria Uno, but then we became despondent and distracted because you can't get food like this at home (at least not in our homes). We decided to take a walk (to think and also to digest). Maybe Chicago's character would come through its streets.

MOODY: A MEANINGFUL NAME
(NOT A MOROSE ATTITUDE)

Walking in downtown Chicago isn't like it used to be. Ten years ago if you took a stroll after dark anywhere in the Loop (so named because this section of the city is encircled by elevated trains, also known as the "El") or the River North section (so named because it's north of the Chicago River), you would be mugged. It was expected. Now, you can walk just about anywhere—in the dark, in the light, whenever you want—thanks to the aforementioned redevelopment and the great number of people walking around (it's true—there's safety in numbers).

We walked west along Chicago Avenue to LaSalle Street, where Moody Bible Institute, one of Chicago's most famous landmarks, stands in all its red-brick grandeur. Founded in 1886 by D. L. Moody, a businessman turned evangelist, Moody (as it's commonly known) has been an important part of the history of Chicago. We also thought the school might hold some clues as to its soul.

As soon as we entered the lobby of the administration building, we were confronted by a dozen eager, enthusiastic high school students from Buffalo. They had traveled to Moody to check out the school and see the city of Chicago. We asked them why Moody? Surely the Buffalo Bible Institute could meet their needs. (We just made that up, so don't try to find it.) One particularly expressive girl seemed to speak for the entire group when she said, "We don't just want to learn the Bible. We want to apply the truth of the Bible

CHICAGO ENDORSES THE TEN COMMANDMENTS

Soon after we left Chicago, we read something that caused us to smile. It also confirmed our thinking that Chicago was a spiritual city. Right before the Chicago Public School System (the nation's largest) was about to resume fall classes, officials gave their blessing to religious groups who wanted to distribute the Ten Commandments to students on book covers.

In an age when most teachers and school administrators are afraid to utter anything remotely religious, Chicago Public Schools CEO Paul Vallas seems absolutely heroic. "I am enthusiastically supportive," he said. "I view the Ten Commandments as history's value statements. They're certainly universally accepted."

The book covers have the Ten Commandments on one side and inspirational quotes from famous figures on the other (there's Mark Twain, John F. Kennedy, and local faves Oprah Winfrey and Michael Jordan). They were paid for by a local religious media group and distributed to churches, synagogues, and community organizations. The executive director of Americans United for the Separation of Church and State made no objection to the book covers.

IT AIN'T NO NEW YORK

Each big city we visited on our search had its own distinct personality. Chicago was no exception. Sometimes it is easier to describe the character of a city by comparison. Perhaps you'll get a feel for how down-to-earth Chicago is if we contrast it with New York City. So, here are our top ten ways to ways to tell if Chicago is your kind of town:

1. **Famous Landmark**
   New York: The Statue of Liberty
   Chicago: Buckingham Fountain

2. **Colorful Part of Town**
   New York: Greenwich Village
   Chicago: The stockyards

3. **Hollywood Connection**
   New York: Woody Allen
   Chicago: Bill Murray

4. **Local Television Celebrity**
   New York: Regis
   Chicago: Oprah

5. **Boss Man**
   New York: George Steinbrenner
   (with apologies to Donald Trump)
   Chicago: Mayor Richard J. Daley

6. **Building Everybody Brags About**
   New York: Empire State Building
   Chicago: The Sears Tower

7. **Famous Slang Expression**
   New York: "Fuhgedaboudit!"
   Chicago: "Cheeseburger! Cheeseburger!"

8. **Most Famous Sports Hero**
   New York: Babe Ruth
   Chicago: Michael Jordan

9. **Famous Local Store**
   New York: Saks
   Chicago: Sears

10. **Most Famous Animal**
    New York: King Kong
    Chicago: Mrs. O'Leary's cow

to the world's hurts. The students of Moody go into the city and the world and make a difference. That's what we want to do."

We could tell from the cheers and high-fives of the other students that they agreed. We wondered aloud what it was about Moody that stirred such passion among these students, none of whom had ever been on the campus before. Then we walked into a room that held the answer, not only to our question, but to the identity and soul of Chicago as well.

The D. L. Moody Museum is an exceptionally well-conceived and executed interactive history of the founder of the Institute. Moody wasn't just some guy they named a school after. From the day he arrived in Chicago in

1856 to the day he died in 1899, he did more to help others find meaning in their lives—spiritually and physically—than anyone else. In 1860 Moody founded a Sunday school for poor children. During the Civil War, he worked among the soldiers. After the Chicago Fire of 1871, Moody ministered to the needs of those left homeless. From 1873–1875, he conducted evangelistic meetings in Great Britain, where he shifted his emphasis from the poor to the middle class. Moody believed that the key to reaching the world for Christ and improving conditions for the downtrodden lay at the feet of those who were able to do something about it. As a result, a group of wealthy young men known as the Cambridge Seven left their careers and went to China as missionaries. Their act of self-sacrifice had an amazing impact on Britain and the United States, especially in the universities.

> "Water runs downhill and the highest hills in America are the great cities. If we can stir them we shall stir the whole country."
> —D. L. Moody, *The History of Evangelism in America*

The legend of the Cambridge Seven grew and eventually led to another meeting organized by Moody in his hometown of Northfield, Massachusetts. Here, at a conference in 1886, a group of students dedicated themselves to reaching the world for Christ. Historians credit this conference as the beginning of the Student Volunteer Movement, which led to one of the greatest expansions of Christianity the world has ever seen. Later that same year, Moody went back to Chicago to establish the school that bears his name.

So what does all of this have to do with Moody Bible Institute and the city of Chicago? Simple. D. L. Moody's passion to inspire others—especially students—to reach the world with a message of hope continues to challenge people more than a hundred years later. In Chicago, all you have to do is walk around, talk to people, and study the history to realize, as we did on this particular day, that the city has been built on a strong foundation of spirituality. There it was. We had our identity.

SPIRITUAL STIRRINGS

Even before we arrived in Chicago, we observed something interesting (at least we thought it was interesting, but we guess you'll be the ultimate judge of that). Here it is:

This was abundantly clear to us as we conducted on-the-street interviews about the meaning of life. In the Northeast, for example, references to God (and even family) were few and far between, but God and family ranked high in the responses once we traveled into the South and Midwest.

There is certainly a Bible Belt in America. We just never assumed that the Belt wrapped around the people of Chicago. It doesn't really (and with all that Chicago-style pizza, there aren't many belts that wrap around the people of Chicago). Chicago isn't known so much as a Bible town as it is known for being a religious one. While traditional values are often lost, or at least diluted, in the other major cities of America, Chicago continues to maintain them.

CATHOLICS IN THE CITY

Once we identified our theme of spirituality for Chicago, we began to notice a strong religious influence in the city. In fact, it surprised us. Perhaps if we had done a little extra preparation and learned a few things in advance, we would have known more about Moody and another very strong spiritual influence in the city—Catholicism.

> **B&S Observation**
>
> THE RELIGIOUS LANDSCAPE OF AMERICA SEEMS TO BE AT ITS HIGHEST PEAK IN THE HEARTLAND, ONLY TO SLOPE OFF AT BOTH COAST-LINES.

Chicago represents the second-largest Catholic population in the U.S. Of course, just having a Catholic population doesn't guarantee that its presence will be felt. (Consider New York, home of the largest Catholic population in the country.) The difference lies in whether people are active in their faith (and this applies to any spiritual group or denomination). That is certainly the case with Catholics in Chicago.

The Catholic Church is steeped in tradition, ceremony, and clerical bureaucracy. But there is some sentiment that the Catholic Church has become irrelevant in the digital age—a notion being dispelled by the Young Adult Ministry (YAM) of the Chicago Archdiocese. This is a group designed for young Catholic adults, married or single, in their twenties and thirties (although we suspect they'd let a Baptist or a Presbyterian join the action). There is one singular focus to YAM: to put people in contact with each other and with programs that respond to their needs. In other words, YAM is trying to integrate faith into everyday life.

We wondered if YAM was just more of the same ancient, traditional, sanctuary-sitting stuff, but its programs sure didn't sound same-old, same-old to us:

Theology on Tap. If you think that the name of this program sounds a bit oxymoronic (like God stuff in a bar), then you are correct. That's exactly what it is. Theology on Tap is a "speaker and conversation" series that takes place every summer at over one hundred parishes in the dioceses of Chicago, Rockford, and Joliet. Adults in their twenties and thirties gather to hear talks and discuss a number of issues.

Last year Theology on Tap had more than two hundred meetings. The topics included relationships, everyday faith, prayer, history, why Catholics do what they do, and many others. The point is this: Many young adults are interested in discussing matters of faith, but they don't always want to enter a cathedral to do it. Theology on Tap isn't afraid to meet them where they are. (The Chicago Archdiocese presents each series in groups of four. We suggested that they do six at a time, and then they could refer to each series as a six-pack.)

Chicago Bummers

Alongside its glorious religious history, Chicago has had its share of tragedy and missteps. Here's a short list of some tragic events:

1871—THE CHICAGO FIRE, allegedly set by a cow kicking over a lantern during a bad dry spell, killed 250 people, left 90,000 homeless, and destroyed one-third of the city.

1919—THE CHICAGO RACE RIOTS led to the death of 38 people and left 1,000 black families homeless.

1929—ST. VALENTINE'S MASSACRE was the name given to Chicago mobster Al Capone's execution of seven members of a rival gang—on Valentine's Day, of course.

1968—THE DEMOCRATIC CONVENTION was overrun by thousands of students who had taken to the streets to protest the Vietnam War. Nobody was killed, but they sure made a mess.

Y.A.C.H.T. Club. While Theology on Tap is what it sounds like, the Y.A.C.H.T. Club isn't. There aren't luxury boats involved, and the only water is of the holy variety. Y.A.C.H.T. Club stands for Young Adult Catholics Hanging Together. It is a monthly gathering of young adults in various restaurant locations throughout Chicagoland. This is another ministry designed to bring people together in a format where they can discuss connections between their lives, their work, and their Catholic faith.

Volunteers in Action. Recognizing that following Christ means serving others, YAM encourages its participants to use their time and talent to help others. It sponsors a Volunteer Fair and has a list of nearly one hundred organizations that are in need of volunteer assistance.

Is YAM a sham, or is it working? Well, from what we could tell, it is bringing the Catholic Church to the people instead of insisting that they come to it. But that's not just our opinion. According to *Chicago* magazine, the Young Adult Ministry's monthly mass at Old Saint Patrick's Church in downtown Chicago is one of the top ten places in the city to meet people.

WHEATON COLLEGE AND THE BILLY GRAHAM CENTER

As you fan out from Chicago in any direction (OK, you can't fan to the east since Lake Michigan blocks your way), you notice an amazing array of religiously based institutions whose influence is felt around the world. Several religious nonprofit organizations are headquartered within the boundaries of Chicagoland. There are more than two thousand churches in Chicago, including the nation's largest. (We'll take a look at it later in the chapter.) A half-dozen religious book publishers and several Christian periodicals call Chicago home. And there are several Christian colleges and universities—both Protestant and Catholic—within an hour's drive of Chicago's city center. We paid a visit to one of the best known.

Wheaton, Illinois is a sleepy college town, but the college named for the Chicago suburb is hardly asleep. Since its beginning in 1860, Wheaton College has been a world force in missions, scholarship, and academics. Was it a coincidence that the school was founded in the same year Moody gave up business for full-time Christian work? Probably, but it's the kind of coincidence that makes even a skeptic wonder about the miracle of God's timing.

Wheaton College has a distinguished list of graduates, but the most famous alumnus has to be Billy Graham. After graduating in 1943, he married fellow graduate Ruth Bell, and the two settled in Chicago, and over the next few years Billy Graham pastored his first church, launched his first radio ministry, and accepted the presidency of a fledgling evangelistic movement called Youth for Christ—all in Chicago. Billy went on to found a worldwide ministry that continues to this day. No one in history has personally preached to more people than Billy Graham (more than a billion, and we're not exaggerating).

In 1980, the Billy Graham Center, located on the campus of Wheaton College, was dedicated to the task of promoting world evangelism. As you enter the impressive Rotunda of Witnesses to start the tour, you find yourself standing in the middle of nine ornate banners proclaiming the images and testimonies of history's greatest Christian saints. Inspired by these stirring words, you continue through a first-class exhibit showing the history of evangelism in America, from the Pilgrims in the seventeenth century to Billy Graham in the present one.

We aren't ones to get misty-eyed over such things, but we've got to be honest here. It was a profound moment. We were beginning to see that spirituality, while a very private matter for each of us, is also part of something much greater than ourselves.

WILLOW CREEK

Thirty miles north of Wheaton is the affluent Chicago suburb of South Barrington. There is a Starbucks, a Lexus dealership, a new Cineplex, and hundreds upon hundreds of beautiful two-story brick homes. Oh, and Willow Creek Community Church, America's largest, is here as well. We didn't meet Bill Hybels, the founding pastor who started the church in a movie theater twenty-five years ago. He's a busy guy and we're just a couple of guys. But we did walk the campus, a hugely impressive layout that includes a five-thousand-seat auditorium, and we talked to a lot of people who know what Willow Creek is all about.

Every weekend more than seventeen thousand people attend six different services at Willow Creek. But these aren't your ordinary church services. There's no pulpit, no robed choir, no candles, no ornamentation of any kind. Before Hybels gives his "talk" (no sermons here, at least not in the traditional sense), a jazz band gets things going. A parade of gifted singers, musicians, and actors present music and drama designed to draw you into a spiritual connection with others and with God.

WGN: The Voice of Chicagoland

Imagine our surprise when we got a call at our hotel room asking us to be guests on the Steve Cochran Show on radio station WGN (720 AM). WGN is the major talk-radio station in all of Chicagoland. We were intimidated yet giddy with excitement. (OK, Bruce was intimidated; Stan was giddy.)

WGN sits right on Michigan Avenue, with a window in the broadcasting booth that looks directly onto the sidewalk. On a slow news day, the show host can simply comment on the appearance and behavior of people walking by. (This doesn't help much in winter when people are bundled up, but the summer heat brings out all sorts of tasteless apparel and excess flesh.)

We arrived early and were escorted into the engineer's room. (We forget the guy's name, but he was the Roz to Steve Cochran's Frasier.) Stan made the mistake of sitting in the engineer's chair (although the fact that it was positioned at the sound board should have been a clue). Stan couldn't help it. He was giddy. The guy yelled at us, and we stayed out of his way and waited without further incident. (OK, there was a slight accident that involved a spilled cup of coffee on some sort of transformer or amplifier. Fortunately, the equipment was turned off, and we were able to sop up the evidence with pages from a phone directory before the engineer guy noticed.)

If radio is theater of the mind, then Steve Cochran is the Steven Spielberg of talk show hosts. We did our search-for-the-meaning-of-life schtick and got great responses from several callers. Steve even gave us his take on the meaning of life, which had something to do with hope and children. We don't exactly remember because we were a little distracted when he was talking. The engineer guy had turned on that amplifier thing, and it started to smoke. We hoped nobody would notice the coffee-soaked phone pages in the wastebasket near where we had been sitting.

We must have done fairly well on the program because they invited us to come back after we had finished our search. We are anxious to do so. (And we aren't afraid of being confronted again by that hostile engineer. We heard that he got fired for spilling coffee on the equipment.)

More than a church, Willow Creek is a community. This is what really impressed us. According to *Christianity Today,* America's leading Christian magazine (published in Chicago, of course), everything at Willow Creek "circles back to small groups—more than 2,600 of them." Here is where the grass roots ministry of Willow Creek takes place. Every one of the small groups is involved in one of the church's hundred-plus ministries. When you think "ministry," don't just think of Bible studies (although those are definitely part of the program). More than a third of the ministries are "community-care programs." There is a divorce-recovery small group (this one has upward of five hundred people), a small group of seven hundred (suddenly these small groups don't seem so small, do they?) that feeds people in Chicago's city center, and a small group that fixes and repairs cars. We even found a small group of three guys (OK, that's small) that does nothing but vacuum the church (there's a lot of carpet in Willow Creek).

The point of all this is that Willow Creek isn't just a place where only the faithful go to insulate themselves from the big bad world. Thousands of ordinary people come every week to share each other's burdens and to do what they can to take the true meaning of the gospel to a world desperate for hope, beginning with their own backyard. (Church staffers estimate that there are still half a million unchurched people living within thirty minutes of the church.)

This is what spirituality is like, Willow Creek style. Clearly, this kind of spirituality—the kind that takes your private faith public—brings tremendous meaning to those who participate. But is this the only kind of spirituality? Do you have to have faith in God in order to find spiritual meaning, or is it possible to find spiritual fulfillment in other ways?

HARPO SPIRITUALITY

There is a new kind of spirituality spreading across America, and we found it in Chicago, right alongside Moody, YAM, Wheaton, and Willow Creek. This new spirituality isn't necessarily more prevalent in Chicago than in the rest of the country, but this is where it originates: from a single place, one hour a day, five days a week, into tens of millions of homes. In fact, we stood at the very spot of what has become a shrine of sorts representing this new spirituality: Harpo Studios.

Harpo is Oprah spelled backward, but there is nothing backward about the vast multimedia empire of Oprah Winfrey that is headquartered in Chicago. She is the CEO and chairwoman of Harpo Productions, Harpo Films, Harpo Studios, Harpo Video, and Harpo Enterprises. She has a significant presence on the Web with On-line With Oprah, and she is part owner of the Oxygen Media cable television network. Most recently, Oprah has joined with the Hearst Corporation to produce *O: The Oprah Magazine.*

What makes Oprah's success so amazing is that she has triumphed in a culture and at a time when the obstacles of being black, poor, and a woman would have ruled many other people out of the game. We knew her life experiences must have given her keen insights about the meaning of life, and we were anxious to hear them. Unfortunately, the Harpo people had never heard of us, so we weren't allowed to enter the studios. (Or, maybe they had heard of us and that's why we were locked out.)

What does Oprah have to do with spirituality? Well, lots, but it's not the kind of spirituality connected to the God of the Bible. Instead, it is a spirituality of inner strength. Oprah doesn't thump a Bible behind a pulpit in church, but she is very clear and direct about her intent to preach a gospel of positivism and inspiration. In fact, her television show was reformatted in 1998 as "change your life television." Toward that end:

- Oprah refers to her show as "a ministry."
- The stories on her show and in her magazine feature women who have a sense of "empowerment."
- As one journalist has reported, the lexicon of spiritual awareness on Oprah's show includes: freeing yourself from the "disease to please"; recognizing that your life is a "journey"; understanding that "the path to self-awareness is what you feel, not what you think"; and discovering "the real you."

The totality of these proclamations has earned Oprah the title, America's Priestess of Positivism. The benchmark of success for any self-respecting priestess is influence. And she has it. Each one of the selections in the Oprah's Book Club has become a bestseller. (She had endorsed twenty-eight titles at the time we visited Chicago.) It has gotten to the point where her target audience—women—look to her for spiritual guidance. One woman who benefited from the Oprah's charitable assistance said, "Someday I'll probably tell my son, 'When you want change, pray to St. Oprah.'"

While we didn't get a chance to speak directly with Oprah, she has clearly and forcefully expressed her opinions about the meaning of life across the television screen, the airwaves, the Web, and in print. From what we can ascertain, her meaning of life is found in a journey of self-discovery that leads to being empowered to be "the real you." It is all about finding the spirit within you.

As a young child Oprah dreamed of becoming a missionary. Her dream came true; she is a tremendous evangelist for her gospel of the inner spirit.

THE SOUL OF THE CITY

We had mixed feelings as we left Chicago and nosed our trusty rental car westward on I-90. The prospect of heading to the West Coast thrilled us in no small measure (even though it would take us a few days to get there), but we were sorry to leave a city we very much enjoy. On previous trips to Chicago our delight had always been tied to great restaurants, a bustling downtown, and friendly, down-to-earth people. Well, we experienced all of that this time, but we also came away with something new. For the first time we valued this city for what it had contributed to our own heritage, especially in the area of spirituality.

When it comes to the meaning of life, most of us will do our best to find it through some outward vehicle. But out of all the things we found as we traveled through thirty states and eleven cities—education, public service, family, and competition, for example—only three of the conduits for meaning focused on the inner part of all of us: passion, spirituality, and love. Of those three, it dawned on us that spirituality is the one quality that forms the taproot for the other two. And it's the three inner qualities together that provide the foundation for the outward expressions. If you were to diagram it out (which we did on a napkin while eating at Fosters Freeze), it would look like the chart on the following page.

We were discovering the things you do and the way you express yourself, if they are to bring meaning to your life, must come out of an inner passion or love. Otherwise you're just going through the motions. Not only that, but your passion and love for what you do and the way you express yourself needs to come out of some root or core of spirituality. This is what Chicago showed us, and that's why we felt such an attachment.

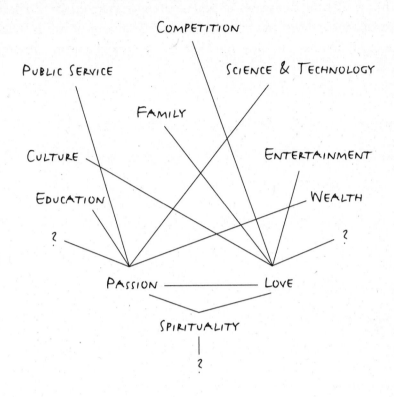

In their book *Bold Purpose,* Dan Allender and Tremper Longman proposed this: "Life must have something more, something that infuses the rest of our existence with significance. . . . For many people, religion becomes a way to cope with life without coming to grips with God."

Substitute the word "spirituality" for "religion," and the question becomes: What kind of spirituality is it? And does it really matter? In Chicago we found people who rooted their spirituality in the God of the Bible. Here they found a belief system and a way of living that gave them hope, while challenging them to help the hurts of others. The people and the institutions we encountered advocated an active spirituality that takes your faith public. We also found a strong strain of spirituality that seeks personal fulfillment without the reference point of a formal system of belief. People who embrace this kind of private spirituality don't exclude God, but they don't necessarily see him as someone who exists apart from them. They believe spiritual fulfillment is within you, and that's where it stays.

So which form of spirituality brings more meaning to your life? We had an idea, but we had been on the road long enough to know that we couldn't come to any conclusions just yet. We knew we were bound to find something new at our next stop.

departure
0 5 2 8 9

NEXT STOP: SEATTLE

8

SEATTLE:

Does Wealth Make Life Worth It?

Everyone needs a hero, someone you admire who can inspire you to greatness. These days people make heroes out of those who get where they are through dumb luck and shameless self-promotion, like that naked *Survivor* guy who won a million dollars. We happen to believe that heroes should be made of better stuff, like the larger-than-life pioneers of days gone by who succeeded because they had determination, courage, and faith (OK, and a little dumb luck).

As we left Chicago and began our journey west, our determination, courage, and faith were running low. (And we weren't having much luck, although we had plenty of the dumb part.) We were two-thirds of the way into our journey, we were running out of clean underwear, and we faced a formidable obstacle before we would reach Seattle, the next city on our tour—namely two thousand miles of open road through nothing but cornfields, prairies, mountains, and Fosters Freeze fast-food stands. We needed a hero—no, two heroes (so each of us would have someone to admire)—to inspire us.

Since we had nothing better to do for the next few days, we ran through a checklist of likely candidates—Sonny & Cher, Martin & Lewis, Barnum & Bailey, Penn & Teller, Sacco & Vanzetti—but none of them seemed right for us. We aren't entertainers, magicians, or Italian immigrants wrongfully accused of murder. We're dreamers! We're explorers! We're two guys with nothing better to do than travel from east to west. That's when it hit us. Nearly two hundred years ago two guys named Lewis & Clark journeyed west across the plains and mountains in search of something significant.

That's exactly what we were doing. We had the inspiration we needed. We had our heroes.

As we thought about it, we uncovered some eerie similarities and crazy contrasts between those legendary explorers and us (kind of like those spooky connections between Presidents Lincoln and Kennedy):

Lewis & Clark left the comforts of a big midwestern city (St. Louis);
Bruce & Stan left the comforts of a big midwestern city (Chicago).

Lewis & Clark were searching for the elusive Northwest Passage;
Bruce & Stan were searching for the elusive Meaning of Life.

Lewis & Clark's expedition was known as the Corps of Discovery;
Bruce & Stan's expedition was known as the Core of Discovery (not really, but that sounds pretty cool, doesn't it?).

Lewis & Clark traveled through Iowa, South Dakota, North Dakota, Montana, Idaho, and Washington on their way to the Pacific Ocean;
Bruce & Stan traveled through Iowa, South Dakota, Montana, Idaho, and Washington on their way to the Pacific Ocean (they avoided North Dakota for obvious reasons).

Lewis & Clark published a journal of their experience, a demanding process that led to Lewis committing suicide;
Bruce & Stan published a journal of their experience, a demanding process that left to their editor wanting to commit suicide.

The miles flew by as we fancied ourselves explorers entering strange and wonderful new territory. (We even stopped at Wall Drug in South Dakota and thought about purchasing a couple of fringed leather coats and coonskin caps, which you can actually buy there, along with enormous pieces of pie and any number of useless trinkets. However, we changed our minds when Bruce tried on the outfit, and a little boy whispered to his mother, "Mommy, look, there's Elton John!") Finally, after three days of relentless driving and endless boredom, our goal was in sight. We could barely contain ourselves when we finally crossed the Cascades and entered America's newest city of dreams: Seattle.

A CITY TOO BEAUTIFUL FOR WORDS

Seattle has always been a beautiful city, with its remarkable combination of water, trees, hills, and mountains. But after traveling for days without seeing a large city of any kind, it was almost too beautiful for words.

After you get on the I-90 bridge, the Seattle skyline looms ahead, and beyond that the dramatic views of Elliot Bay and Puget Sound. We camped out on Lake Union just north of downtown (OK, so we splurged and got a Courtyard), which proved to be a great location. South and west of us were historic Pioneer Square and the famous Pike Place Market; directly west was the Seattle Center, home of the 1962 World's Fair and Seattle's defining landmark, the Space Needle; a little to the north and west we could see Queen Anne Hill; and over the hill to the north and east of us was the University of Washington. It was all very cool.

We say that because Seattle is the city of cool. New York may be sophisticated, and New Orleans is funky, but Seattle is just plain cool. Part of it has to do with the scenery, but a lot of it revolves around the lifestyle. The people here seem young, fit, creative, and laid back in a recreational and ambitious sort of way. And every single one of them is drinking coffee, usually in a café like the one on *Frasier,* or they are gathered in a group around a sidewalk table under an umbrella with the name "Starbucks" or "Pellegrino" emblazoned on it.

COFFEE CULTURE CLUB

The coffee culture has invaded every corner of society. (We know this is true because we saw a Starbucks in Billings, Montana, right next to Al's Bait & Tackle Shop. Come to think of it, the Starbucks was *in* Al's Bait & Tackle Shop.) But it started right here in Seattle. You can credit Howard Schultz, Starbucks CEO, for getting the whole bean . . . er, ball . . . going. While in Italy in the early 1980s, he noticed that the entire culture revolved around coffee—strong coffee, not the weak coffee shop coffee America was used to. Schultz brought his experience back to his hometown of Seattle and convinced two brothers who operated a wholesale coffee company to open up a European-style café. Taking his cue from a coffee-drinking character named Starbuck in the novel *Moby Dick*, Schultz put up a sign and a legend of American enterprise and lifestyle was born. In less than two decades, Starbucks has expanded from a single location in Seattle to more than 3,800 worldwide.

"I'LL TELL YOU WHAT YOUR THEME FOR SEATTLE SHOULD BE . . ."

Don't believe the Chamber of Commerce reports that the weather in Seattle is drizzly and overcast for 360 days of the year. If that statistic is correct, then we hit Seattle on its only five days of sunshine for the year. The weather was beautiful and we were anxious to enjoy it.

We went to our Seattle file and pulled out the "People Who Don't Know Us, But We Know Somebody Who Knows Them" list. We scanned the names (and the sketchy biographical info) for someone who met three criteria:

A. They must own a house on the water, so we could enjoy the scenic vistas of Seattle;

B. They must have a boat, so we could spend the afternoon sailing on Seattle's waterways; and

C. They must be gullible enough to invite us over.

Seattle CityFacts

FOUNDED: 1851
POPULATION: 536,978
METRO: 3,320,829
NICKNAME: The Jewel of the Pacific Northwest
BUT WE CALL IT: The only place where jewels don't impress
KNOWN FOR: Rain, Boeing, Microsoft, Starbucks, the Space Needle, and more rain
FAMOUS NATIVES: Carol Channing, Bill Gates, Jimi Hendrix, Gypsy Rose Lee

Bill and Maggie fit the profile perfectly—especially criterion "C." We called and made our pitch, they bought it, and we had our invitation.

Bill and Maggie gave us directions to their house on the north shore of Mercer Island. (We already knew it was on the waterfront because we looked it up on the map before calling them to ensure that they met criterion "A.") We were a little worried at first because the I-90 freeway goes across the north end of Mercer Island, and it looked like they might be living under the off ramp. But the road curved, and we found their house around a secluded bend. The house was more impressive than we had expected. They escorted us into their living room, where the north-facing wall consists of windows that were thirty feet high, revealing a view of their sport court, boat dock, and Lake Washington. (Yessiree, we could get used to this Seattle lifestyle.)

We felt obligated to chat with Bill and Maggie for a few minutes before we asked them to take us out on the lake in their boat. Since we had nothing in common with them, we just talked about our search for the meaning of life. We were describing how we had found a theme for each of the cities we had visited, and we were just about to admit that we had no theme for Seattle when Maggie interrupted us. "I'll tell you what your theme for Seattle should be: Wealth!"

To prove her point, Maggie whipped out the prior month's issue of *Town & Country* magazine (a kind of *People* magazine for the wealthy) with the cover story about Seattle's cyber rich (those people who became multimillionaires in the digital boom of the last decade). The article examined "how they live, what they care about, and what they are doing with their fast-made fortunes." The *Town & Country* reporters didn't have to look too hard to find people to interview for their articles. There are sixty thousand households in the Puget Sound area with a net worth of $1 million or higher.

To further prove her point, Maggie and Bill took us out on the lake in their boat to look at the homes of the rich and super rich. (Our plan was unfolding perfectly. They were playing right into our hands. Now, we only needed to devise a scheme to get them to invite us to dinner.) Our hosts were the perfect couple to take us on this cruise to view the affluence of Seattle. As captain, Bill navigated the boat in silence, while Maggie (his first mate, literally) gave a running narration of who lived in each home and how they acquired their wealth. We spent several hours sailing along the shoreline of Lake Washington (all 48 miles of it) on that beautiful day. Along the way we passed mansions owned by two guys you may have heard of.

Microsoft chairman, Bill Gates. The Gates compound is on the eastern shore of Lake Washington in the suburb of Medina. While most of the homes are built on large lots, the Gates compound is built into the hillside and it is roughly the width of a small town. When you consider that the publicized cost estimate was $50 million, its appearance isn't too ostentatious. But most of the house is obscured from view by the forest planted in front of it. (The trees make it impossible for paparazzi in helicopters to get too close.) We floated in front of the house for quite a while, hoping to get a glimpse of someone through the binoculars. Stan swears he saw an iMac on the kitchen sink.

Microsoft cofounder, Paul Allen. We could see Paul Allen's house long before we floated in front of it. It isn't hard to miss. It is the only house on the lake that has an adjoining concert hall (he needs a place for his rock-star musician friends to perform). The concert hall is huge, but it isn't very noticeable because the gigantic floating helicopter pad distracts your attention. This is a stark-white, two-story, flat-top barge about the size of a municipal parking lot. It reminded us of something from a James Bond movie. We told Bill to keep our boat moving along because we expected commandos in wet suits with daggers in their mouths and spear guns in their hands to swim from under that monstrosity and commandeer our boat if we didn't leave the area.

By the time we completed our mansion-viewing voyage (with a brief pass by the University of Washington at the northwest end of the lake), it was time for dinner. (We had timed it perfectly!) We pulled the boat into a neighborhood marina and ate dinner on the outdoor patio of one of the restaurants. It was a fitting place to talk further with Bill and Maggie about the affluence that exists in Seattle, and particularly about the philosophy these newly minted multimillionaires have about money.

Back at our hotel that evening, we knew that wealth and financial prosperity would be a fitting theme for Seattle. We made a list of the questions we could ask people to discover how money plays into the meaning of life:

- Can the meaning of life be found in money?
- Does your perspective about the meaning of life change as your net worth increases?
- Does money give you security?
- Is significant meaning found in using your money for the benefit of others?

We knew we would never have to worry about where to go to purchase a floating helicopter pad, but these questions seemed to have universal application regardless of a person's tax bracket or net worth. Most people in America don't have the seven-figure incomes of the residents in the exclusive homes we viewed. (Our own annual incomes are seven figures, but two of those digits are on the right side of the decimal point.) Nonetheless, these questions about money and the meaning of life seem to apply to everyone. Sometimes, money is an even greater influence on your life if you don't have much of it. We had the right questions to ask. Now we had to find the people who could give us answers.

THE WEIGHT OF WEALTH

The figures are staggering. The United States is the richest nation on earth, and not just by a slim margin. Looking at the economy in terms of market value, American companies are collectively worth six times more than the companies in the United Kingdom or Japan, and almost fourteen times more

SEATTLE MASS TRANSIT: BACK TO THE FUTURE

In Seattle on any given day, it is possible to take several forms of transportation. You can drive, of course (and many people do, enough to seriously clog the freeways and bridges with their Beemers and Volvo Cross Country wagons), you can ride a bike, and you can take a ferryboat. Or you can use Seattle's version of mass transit, although we wouldn't advise it. The New York subways are quick, the Washington Metro is a dream, and Chicago's El is very functional; but Seattle's form of mass transit is more like a ride than an efficient form of moving people from one point to another. They call it the monorail, but don't get any ideas that you're going to travel at Disney World–like speed. You should be so lucky.

The Seattle monorail was built for Century 21, the 1962 World's Fair (so it really was a ride). This bus-on-a-rail runs from the Space Needle at the Seattle Center to downtown, a distance of about a mile. This may have been a marvel of modern mass transit and a sneak peak into the future back in 1962, but now that we're actually in the twenty-first century, it's a museum piece. In the time it takes to pay the fare, board the train, and ride at a snail's pace to the downtown area, you can walk it with time left over for a cup of coffee.

than the companies in Germany. There are 2.5 million millionaires and more than 250 billionaires in the U.S., far more than any other nation.

Not only are Americans the richest people on the planet, they are also the most generous. According to a *Time* magazine cover story on philanthropy (which hit the newsstands during our trip), three-quarters of all Americans gave money to charity in 1999, compared to 43 percent of the French and 44 percent of the Germans. Total charitable giving in 1999 totaled $190 billion, the highest level in three decades.

Although the largest percentage of giving comes from people writing small checks on a regular basis, it's the big donations and the big donors who grab headlines. Ted Turner made news a few years ago when he pledged $1 billion to the United Nations. Financier George Soros of New York has given away $2 billion to several public health, education, and cultural programs. But the granddaddy of all givers is Seattle's own Bill Gates. By most accounts, the founder of Microsoft is worth somewhere between $50 and $65 billion (depending on the price of Microsoft stock), a nearly incomprehensible figure. But consider this. Gates, who has vowed to give his entire fortune away in his lifetime, has endowed the Bill and Melinda Gates Foundation to the tune of $22 billion, making it the world's largest philanthropic organization. The goal of the foundation is to give away $1 billion per year. [Note to selves: Learn how to write a grant proposal and submit it to the Bill and Melinda Gates Foundation.]

According to *Time,* Gates has given away more money faster than anyone else in history. He has been compared to such legendary tycoon/philanthropist types as Andrew Carnegie and John D. Rockefeller, who used their incredible wealth to fund libraries, hospitals, and universities a hundred years ago. (In an ironic twist, the Gates foundation is currently funding efforts to wire some of the very same libraries built by Carnegie to twenty-first century broadband standards.)

There's no question that Gates's generosity has raised the bar for Seattle's new rich. Pamela Fiori, editor-in-chief of *Town & Country,* reports that many of these Seattle millionaires "are now figuring out creative ways to disseminate their money to causes that have some real meaning for them." So you could say that Seattle is not only the wealth capital of the world, but the giving capital as well.

Many of the so-called "Microsoft millionaires" (there are thousands of them) have retired—often in their thirties and forties—in order to "pursue their own passions." That usually includes collecting and enjoying expensive homes, art, and various implements of transportation. But some of these wealthy people have so much money that the time they spend collecting stuff pales in comparison to the time they spend giving their wealth away.

Why are the high-tech rich so anxious to give away their money? One Seattle philanthropist summarized it this way: There is a basic need in people to share what they have with others. Your willingness to give part of your candy bar away as a kid isn't that far removed from a millionaire's desire to share his or her wealth. In addition, the principle that "it is better to give than to receive" really is true. "I don't enjoy spending money that much," the philanthropist said, "but I really enjoy putting it to work for good causes."

> "Seattle is the epicenter of philanthropy. It couldn't be a more exciting environment."
> —Doug Picha, Children's Hospital Foundation

A TALE OF TWO GIVERS

Bill Gates and Paul Allen have a lot in common. They are both from Seattle, they cofounded Microsoft, they live a few miles apart, and between them they have a net worth that exceeds the GNP of most nations. But when it comes to charitable giving, they are as far apart as two of the world's richest men can be. Gates has directed billions of dollars to causes such as the immunization of children in Africa, women's reproductive rights, and education. Allen has given hundreds of millions to rock and roll and space-alien hunters.

While Gates contributed $750 million to a global children's vaccination program, Allen gave $100 million toward building the Experience Music Project, the $240 million Frank Gehry designed monument to rock. (We toured the EMP, which is an interactive museum contained in a multicolored, amorphous, stainless-steel encased building unlike anything else in Seattle or the world. The centerpiece of this shrine is an exhibit on Jimi Hendrix, one of Paul Allen's heroes.) While Gates gave $1 billion for scholarships, Allen contributed $11 million to the Search for Extraterrestrial Intelligence, also known as SETI. (To his credit, Allen has also contributed to scholarships and art museums in Seattle.)

THE YOUNG AND THE RESTLESS

When people refer to "old money" in Seattle, they are usually referring to people in their fifties and sixties, such as our friends on Mercer Island, who made money the "old-fashioned way"—by building, manufacturing, or investing over a period of many years. Old money traditionally serves on nonprofit boards and gives to civic causes, such as the opera or an art museum. "New money" in Seattle refers to the Microsoft millionaire types in their thirties and forties who joined a company at the right time, rode the tech rocket to success, then cashed out their stock options—all in a relatively short period of time. New money has shown a pattern of giving to education, health, and literacy causes (and occasionally to unique and sometimes controversial programs like Paul Allen's Experience Music Project).

HEDGING THEIR BETS

Some of the tech millionaires are reluctant to take the charity plunge because the jury is still out on their companies. Take the case of Seattle resident Jeff Bezos, founder and CEO of Amazon.com. (His personal stock worth soared to more than $10 billion before Amazon shares dropped like a hardback book off a desk.) Bezos admitted to *Town & Country* that he "had been thinking about philanthropy" but only if his company makes it in the long haul. "I mean, any wealth I have is in Amazon.com stock," he said. "And it goes away the second we stop doing a good job for our customers."

So you've got the old money and the new money in Seattle and other cities across the country. What about the young working class who have arrived a little late for the join-a-tech-company-and-get-rich-quick plan? What kind of attitude do they have toward money and success? That's what we wanted to find out.

We took the ferry to Bainbridge to meet with Steven Screen, a communications manager and media consultant in his late twenties. Steven shares an office with his father, who, coincidentally, specializes in teaching nonprofit organizations how to raise significant amounts of money. We talked to Steven first, because we wanted to get some insights into the mind-set of people in their twenties when it comes to money and giving.

Steven explained to us that the attitude he sees among his peers is that

Watch for Flying Fish

We saw a few great shows while we were on our search. One was on Broadway, one was off-Broadway, one was in Las Vegas, and one was at the Pike Place Fish Market in Seattle. Pike Place is an open-air marketplace for artists and vendors hocking everything from fresh vegetables to handcrafted wooden neckties. The most famous part of the marketplace is the Fish Market where fish flinging has become a tourist attraction.

There are huge displays of dead (and nearly dead) fish on ice at the market. If you walk by, you'll be drawn into a conversation with one of the employees, most likely dressed in fluorescent-orange rubber bib overalls (there's nothing inconspicuous about the Fish Market). If you order a fish, say a twelve-pound sockeye salmon, you don't get the one lying on the ice in front of you. Oh no, that would be much too mundane for the Pike Place Fish Market. Instead, someone from the back of the market flings your fish a distance of twenty feet through the air to another fish guy in front of the counter, who catches your beauty and wraps it in paper, all in one motion, to the delight of dozens of camera-toting tourists.

The Pike Place Fish Market has brought the fun back to dead fish. And they are famous for more than just the flinging part. They have a reputation as one of the premier businesses for employee loyalty and customer satisfaction. They even produce corporate training videos. Successful companies like Alaska Airlines, Marriott, and Sprint have studied their techniques.

We asked one of those rubber-suited fishmongers about the meaning of life. He beamed and gave us the company line: "The meaning of life is all about enjoying life and enjoying work." And then he added what must have been his own personal philosophy, " . . . and procreation." We weren't sure whether he was referring to fish or humans, but we wanted to leave before a twelve-pound infant came flying through the air.

work should be part of your life, but it shouldn't be your life. It used to be that people worked into their later years and then retired. Now people are trying to do as little as they can for as much as they can just so they can "retire" in their thirties and forties. He quoted Earl Palmer, pastor of Seattle's University Presbyterian Church: "You are not designed to retire. God wants you to be active." Part of that activity needs to include volunteerism, or it could be a career built around service to others.

We discovered that most members of the young working class haven't jumped on the charity bandwagon yet, at least not in the way the old or new rich have. "People my age are very skeptical," Steven said. "They've been preached at and marketed to all their lives, and they just aren't listening. If you try to tell me what is valuable and what I should do, I will immediately stop listening. Give me the outcome of what you're proposing, and then let me make the judgment as to whether it's valuable or not."

In addition to being skeptical, these young workers are very results and outcome oriented. They don't want to invest themselves in something that's impossible or difficult to measure. They want to be able to quantify the result. "My peers are more inclined to contribute their skills and their time rather than give their money away," said Steven. "You build a set of skills through your work, and then you get involved in the community by applying your skills to something that matters to you. If you can't do that, then neither your work nor your giving will be meaningful to you."

Now Steven was touching on something meaningful to us: the meaning of life. We pressed him for more. "So are you saying that you and your peers find more meaning in giving their time and their skills than in giving their money away?"

"Helping others with your time and your skills in a way that produces results is meaningful," Steven quickly replied, "but only as you build relationships with the people you are helping. Let me summarize it for you relative to helping a nonprofit organization." We were enthralled by what this young man was saying. Not only did we take copious notes, but we put his summary in bold print, kind of like this:

IF YOU CAN PRODUCE THE RESULT WHILE
GETTING THE SATISFACTION
OF USING YOUR SKILL SET TO HELP THE ORGANIZATION,

AND YOU BUILD THE RELATIONSHIP WITH THE
PEOPLE THE ORGANIZATION SERVES,
AND YOU GET THE RESPECT OF THE PEOPLE
YOU ARE HELPING—
THEN YOU'VE HIT A GRAND SLAM.

LATE NIGHT AT GOLDEN GARDENS

Steven invited us to attend a gathering of twenty-somethings from University Pres at Golden Gardens, a popular Seattle beach where various groups of people build bonfires on weekend nights and do what people do when they stand around a big fire. We talked to several of the forty or so students, grad students, and working professionals who were there to connect with each other and share stories about their journeys of faith (the people gathered around the bonfire next to ours were celebrating some kind of pagan ritual). As you might expect, we asked them to tell us about the meaning of life, especially as it relates to wealth, and here are some of the responses:

THERE'S A LOT OF WEALTH IN SEATTLE. I REALIZED A LITTLE WHILE AGO THAT THE WEALTH HERE AND IN AMERICA IS A LITTLE OSTENTATIOUS, AND THAT THERE'S MORE TO LIFE THAN CHASING AFTER THE ALMIGHTY DOL-LAR. THE THINGS THAT ARE FREE—FRIENDS, HIKES, VOL-UNTEERING YOUR TIME—ARE MUCH MORE MEANINGFUL THAN HAVING A LOT OF MONEY. —SARAH, DOCUMENTARY FILMMAKER

AS FOR THE WEALTH QUESTION, MY OBSERVATION IS THAT WEALTHY PEOPLE ARE JUST AS GENEROUS AS POOR PEOPLE. —JIM, ATTORNEY

YOU SHOULD USE THE GIFTS YOU HAVE TO HELP OTHERS, CONTRIBUTE TO SOCIETY, AND MAKE THE WORLD A BETTER PLACE. I WANT TO MAKE A CONTRIBUTION THAT LASTS BEYOND MY LIFETIME. —MARK, MEDICAL STUDENT, UNIVERSITY OF WASHINGTON

IT'S ONE THING TO SAY YOU KNOW WHAT THE MEANING
OF LIFE IS, AND ANOTHER THING TO DO IT. WHATEVER YOU
DO, IT'S IMPORTANT TO SEE THE EFFECT OF YOUR WORK ON
THE LIVES OF OTHER PEOPLE. —LAURIANNE, GRADUATE
STUDENT

IN MY SEARCH FOR THE MEANING OF LIFE, I BECAME A
CHRISTIAN. THAT WAS TWO YEARS AGO. NOW MY MEAN-
ING IS TO FOLLOW GOD, TO FIND ETERNITY, AND TO WALK
WITH JESUS. IN THIS SOCIETY EVERYBODY IS LOOKING FOR
MONEY, POWER, AND SOCIAL STATUS, BUT THERE IS SOME-
THING MORE IMPORTANT. HELPING OTHERS MAKES YOUR
LIFE MORE MEANINGFUL. —CHUN, GRADUATE STUDENT

AN INTERESTING VIEW FROM QUEEN ANNE HILL

We spent our last dinner in Seattle on the porch of a home in the stately
neighborhood of Queen Anne Hill. It lies just to the west of the Space Needle
and is known for its elegant mansions with views of the downtown skyscrapers, Mount Rainier, and Puget Sound on one side, and Lake Union on the
other. Most of the homes in this neighborhood were built around 1919, and
their architecture reflects a refinement and dignity of that historical era. We
were eating and talking with George, a project manager for construction and
renovation projects throughout the Seattle area. You'd use George's company
if you were going to convert a Queen Anne mansion into upscale condos.

Because he is the on-site supervisor of each project, George meets with the
management staff of his clients. He knows the young executives of these companies, including those high-tech startups that have made the big bucks. He
knows what they think about spending money. Through his business relationships, George has become a sort of spiritual counselor to many Seattle execs.
They sense, as did we, that he has a spiritual dimension that gives him balance
in his life—an element sadly lacking in the lives many of the corporate elite.

George told us that he is just old enough to have been around for a few
years before the major high-tech money brought rapid prosperity to Seattle.
Since that time he has witnessed a progression in people's attitudes toward
money.

In the 1970s, college grads went into fields of education or law because they wanted to change the world. Money was not really a factor in their choice of occupation. They were more concerned with helping society.

With the burgeoning prosperity of the 1980s, there was a motivational shift. College grads didn't go into education because there wasn't enough money in it. They still went into law, but not for the purpose of joining public-interest agencies to change the world; instead, they joined major law firms to make the big salaries.

In the 1990s, the monetary success of the tech industry intensified the financial pressure in all career fields. The prevailing mentality was that you had to make lots of money while you could because the opportunity might soon be over.

We sensed a critical tone as he discussed this emphasis on earning power. We suggested that this was nothing more than the old Protestant work ethic: Make hay while the sun shines. We asked him, "Isn't this the industrious, hard-working spirit that has made America great?" George said we were missing the point.

"There has always been a spirit of hard work in America, but it is the motivation that has changed," he said. "For many people, it is no longer a matter of working hard because you enjoy it or for of the benefit to others. Instead, people are choosing their work solely on where the money is. Money is the ultimate goal. They have no other way of keeping score in life except by their money."

According to George, this intense focus on the acquisition of immediate wealth has resulted in an entire generation that has lost the appreciation of delayed gratification. If they want something, they have to have it now!

"When money is the ultimate goal," he continued, "then people mistakenly believe that it can be the solution to all of their problems." George gave us a few examples. "If your marriage is in trouble because you ignored your spouse and children when you were working hard to earn lots of money, then you would be tempted to use money to buy your way out of trouble." We were thinking of the stereotype of a box of candy or a dozen roses. He said we weren't thinking with a Seattle mentality. "In this town, you buy yourself out of trouble by getting your family a new house. That is the biggest 'Get Out of Jail Free' card there is."

As he talked, we thought back to the group we met the night before on the beach at Golden Gardens. They didn't seem to be driven by the almighty dollar. We asked George how they fit into picture. "There is a significant shift back to the middle of the spectrum," he said. "Many younger adults say that they find no appeal in accumulating vast amounts of wealth. Some of them sense an emptiness in that pursuit. Others simply realize that they won't have the opportunity to hit it really big, really soon."

When it was time to go (meaning all the dessert had been consumed), we cut to the bottom line. "So, what is your perspective on money and the meaning of life?" we asked. He didn't hesitate with his answer. "Those people who are motivated by the enjoyment and the challenge of their jobs—and who are not focused on the money—seem to have more meaning in their lives. You actually gain power by having an attitude of indifference about money."

THE SOUL OF THE CITY

As we wrapped up our visit to Seattle, we added one more item to our list of cool things in Seattle: its attitude toward wealth. Wealth is pervasive in Seattle, but the people don't flaunt it. They are casual about it, even understated. You might think that tremendous economic prosperity would lead to gluttonous materialism, but that doesn't appear to be the case in Seattle. Here the people are more into functionality and purpose than status.

The trappings of the wealthy are modest, relatively speaking. Rather than Armani suits, the uniform of the super rich seems to be a golf shirt and Dockers, or a pinpoint Oxford blouse and khaki slacks. They seem to have captured the essence of Aristotle's distinction between needs and wants. Although they have the money to buy their wants, they have the discipline to avoid unrestrained and excessive consumerism. (Of course, their needs are relative and within the context of a multimillionaire's reality. They may not spend $45,000 on a Corvette because that is frivolous or $120,000 on a Mercedes sedan because that would be conspicuous, but they will spend $60,000 on a Range Rover because it is necessary transportation for taking the kids to soccer practice.)

The city seems to have achieved a healthy perspective about wealth, and it seemed to us that this balanced outlook is attributable to individuals—all across the net worth spectrum—who have learned how money fits into the meaning of life.

At the top end, you have the Bill Gates types who have made philanthropy a priority in their lives. These people are not working and living for the sake of money. It has come as the result of what they have done because of the challenge or the enjoyment. And money brings meaning to their life, not by its accumulation, but by using it to assist others and to benefit society.

At the other end of the spectrum are the types we met at Golden Gardens, those bright, hard-working, well-intentioned young professionals who know it is unlikely that they will ever make it to the financial stratosphere. But they have managed to keep a healthy attitude toward wealth, and they don't appear to be envious of those who have so much of it. And even within their limited financial resources, these young professionals recognize the importance of philanthropy in their lives; they consider it a key component of how they use their money and their time.

This is not to say that everyone in Seattle has a balanced perspective about their balance sheet. Some people have placed a priority on wealth that is out of whack. They have a sense of urgency and compulsion to acquire wealth as a status symbol, an aphrodisiac, or an ultimate goal. But it was our impression that these people are in the minority, and there is no lack of role models around them to exemplify a healthy attitude about wealth.

> "Americans are seeking something more meaningful, deeper and healthier. I think it stems in part from what they perceive to be a failure of materialism in [the 20th] century and the fact that there are so many problems that surround us without apparent solutions."
>
> —*George Gallup, Jr.*

Someone we talked to in Seattle suggested that the community has discovered the secret of contentment. It was explained to us that the meaning of "contentment" comes from two Greek words that convey the thought of "self-sufficiency," but not in terms of being a self-made person. Rather, self is not the origin or source of the sufficiency; instead, self is merely the place where the sense of sufficiency resides.

Someone else said that Seattle has an attitude about money that fits Martin Luther's description of the "third conversion." We nodded in agreement to avoid revealing the paucity of our knowledge about Martin Luther, but we had no idea what the person was talking about. Apparently our head nodding was invalidated by the glazed look in our eyes, because the person took the time to explain the context of his statement. "Martin Luther said the 'first conversion' takes place in the mind; the 'second conversion' takes place in the heart; but you know the transformation has really occurred with the 'third conversion' that affects your pocketbook."

Some call it "contentment" and some call it "a third conversion." We just call it knowing how money fits into the meaning of life—knowing that it is not a satisfying object of greed, but an effective tool for doing good. Whatever you call it, Seattle has it.

departure
07618

NEXT STOP: SILICON VALLEY

9

SILICON VALLEY:
Improving Life Through Science & Technology

From Seattle we headed south toward our next stop: the San Francisco Bay Area. Of course, that required driving through Oregon, and we noticed an unmistakable contrast between Oregon's northern and southern borders. On the north end, there appeared to be a spirit of peaceful congeniality between Washington and Oregon. The business owners and residents of each state spoke kindly of their counterparts across the border. The boundary line between the two states was nothing more than an arbitrary geographic demarcation. It's much like the friendly relationship between Canada and United States (except that the people in Oregon don't get stuck with funny coins and currency from Washington that are useless when they return home).

Any spirit of affable coexistence quickly dissipated, however, as we drove through southern Oregon and approached California. Apparently, Oregonians don't look too kindly upon their neighbors to the south. In fact, we detected some outright hostility. Even we—two road-weary cultural observers—could pick up on the subtle clues, like the gigantic billboard that read:

DON'T CALIFORNICATE OREGON!

The Oregon residents complained to us that people from California are arrogant and phony (they said this even though they knew we were from California). We didn't know about the phoniness, but as we entered the San Francisco Bay Area we did perceive an attitude that could be misconstrued as arrogance. Personally, we found it not so much arrogance as it was a mind-set of self-confidence. Arrogance is unwarranted pride; self-confidence, on the other hand, is the assurance that comes from knowing that you have what it takes. In the Bay Area, they've got self-confidence because they know they can discover or invent anything (and if they can't, then we don't need it).

FROM "BAGHDAD BY THE BAY . . ."

Until the last two decades, the city of San Francisco has been the defining feature of the Bay Area. Actually, there are eight counties and several large cities on or near this ocean inlet of 450 square miles. San Francisco has less than 10 percent of the Bay Area's 5 million people, but every other city around the Bay pales in comparison. People who live in San Francisco act as if the other cities don't even exist. In fact, residents throughout all of northern California simply and respectfully refer to San Francisco as "the City." The rest of the world refers to it as "Baghdad by the Bay," an endearing (but somewhat derisive) term coined by legendary *San Francisco Chronicle* columnist Herb Caen.

San Francisco CityFacts

FOUNDED: 1776
CITY POPULATION: 745,774
BAY AREA: 5 million
NICKNAME: City by the Bay
BUT WE CALL IT: City North of the Techies
KNOWN FOR: Cable cars, fog, Golden Gate Bridge, Alcatraz, Fisherman's Wharf
FAMOUS NATIVES: Clint Eastwood, Robert Frost, William Randolph Hearst, Johnny Mathis, O. J. Simpson

San Francisco also enjoys the scenic envy of the other Bay Area cities. The shipyards of Oakland or the landfills of Alviso just can't compete with the postcard views of San Francisco, with its charming cable cars, imaginative skyline, and beautiful bridges, not to mention the incredible array of restaurants and shopping. Whether you're from Omaha or Osaka, you just can't resist the lure of San Francisco.

An important thing you must realize about the San Francisco Bay Area is that it is in Northern California. By contrast, Los Angeles is in Southern California. Now it's true that Rand McNally doesn't recognize California as two states, like the Carolinas or the Dakotas. But try telling that to a resident of California. You see, Californians identify themselves by the polarity of their allegiance to either Northern or Southern California. You might as well chop the state in half, somewhere on the latitude of Fresno. If you live in the northern half, you identify with San Francisco and despise all things associated with the self-absorbed Southern California culture. If you live in the southern half, your affiliation is with the beach and Hollywood, and you abhor the uncouth barbarians who live in the uncivilized north. (Incidentally, both halves want to disassociate themselves from Fresno.)

. . . TO "THE SILICON VALLEY"

San Francisco may be the dominant feature of the Bay Area, but it is no longer the single driving force. A transformation occurred rather suddenly in the late 1970s and early 1980s that shifted the balance of economic power from the City to the Silicon Valley, a geographic area south of San Francisco that runs along the western edge of San Francisco Bay from Stanford University to San Jose. In a nutshell, the landmarks and distinctions of the Bay Area changed dramatically and drastically with the birth of the personal computer. The microprocessor suddenly replaced the Golden Gate Bridge as the symbol of the region. When people talked about bytes, they were no longer referring to the famous sourdough French bread from Fisherman's Wharf.

San Jose claims to be the capital of Silicon Valley. It's the biggest city by far (in fact, San Jose is the largest city in the Bay Area and the eleventh largest in the country). San Jose also has the distinction of having its own song; although "Do You Know the Way to San Jose?" speaks more of its former obscurity than of anything romantic like, "I Left My Heart In San Francisco." Relatively unknown to the rest of the world before the advent of the microprocessor, San Jose's only claim to fame was a Ford Motor manufacturing plant and a bunch of plum orchards. (The county's Chamber of Commerce used the slogan: "Our Fords and Prunes keep the world going." Far from high-tech.)

San Jose CityFacts — San Jose

FOUNDED: 1777
CITY POPULATION: 861,284
BAY AREA: 5 million
NICKNAME: The Heart of Silicon Valley
BUT WE CALL IT: Nice Place to Visit, But You Can't Afford to Live Here
KNOWN FOR: Computer industry
FAMOUS NATIVES: Chuck Berry, Cesar Chavez, Peggy Fleming, Jim Plunkett

Then in 1977, a couple of college dropouts by the names of Steven Jobs and Stephen Wozniak, who tinkered with electronics in Jobs's garage in the San Jose suburb of Los Altos, introduced the Apple II—the world's first personal computer. The computer industry was already part of the landscape around San Jose—Hewlett-Packard was founded by two Stanford engineers in 1939, and in 1970 the Xerox Corporation created the Palo Alto Research Center (PARC) for the purpose of computer and electronics research. But it was the boys from Apple who launched the Silicon Valley revolution.

WHY SILICON VALLEY?

What's the big deal about silicon? Well, it's a semimetallic element, and it just happens to be the second most common element on earth (next to oxygen). What makes silicon useful is that it is a semiconductor, which means it is capable of both conducting and insulating electricity. The heart of any computer is the microprocessor, comprised of many circuit elements fabricated on silicon.

The personal computer created an industry that would reshape the world in profound ways. San Jose and Silicon Valley became—and remain to this day—the high-tech center of the world. There are currently more than three thousand high-tech companies in the Silicon Valley, including some of the best-known in the world. Apple Computers is headquartered in Cupertino, Hewlett-Packard is still in Palo Alto, Sun Microsystems calls Mountain View home, Oracle is in Redwood Shores, while Intel's main office is in Santa Clara.

One-half of the leading venture-capital firms in the world are located in Silicon Valley, mostly to respond to and fund an industry that shows no signs of letting up anytime soon. So why do so many people come here in search of the high-tech Holy Grail? The proximity of Stanford University and the University of California at Berkeley and their super-smart graduates certainly helps, but the Valley generates its own mystique. "It's all about the buzz," said one budding high-tech entrepreneur in a recent *Time* magazine cover story on Silicon Valley. "I can't explain it. It's like magic."

BEYOND THE MAGIC

It would be easy to conclude that there is no explanation for why Silicon Valley has become so successful. It's as if all of these companies and technological advances came out of nowhere, and now that they're all here, the San Francisco Bay Area and Silicon Valley have become breeding grounds for even more high-tech magic. But it just isn't that simple. There's a reason for the success, and we think we found it.

There's more going on than technology in this storied region. In fact, in many ways technology is just the end result of a much larger process. It's one thing to come up with the next generation of microprocessors, capable of computing twice as fast as the last generation, and quite another to think about ways to improve the quality of life for people. Technology provides the means to do certain tasks better and faster. But before you get to the means, you must first consider the meaning of what you're doing, which involves asking a lot of "Why" questions: Why do people need more time? Why do we need more gadgets to help them? Why do you need more time, and what can you do about it?

As we looked for the reason why the Silicon Valley is thriving, we were really searching for the meaning of it all. Like any good students (we're students of meaning), we decided to track down some professors. We paid a visit to the University of California at Berkeley.

UC Berkeley has a lofty reputation for producing world-class scientists. The way we figured it, if technology is the means to the end of producing better and faster stuff, then science is the beginning. Science leads to technology, science opens doors for technology, and science makes technology possible. Technology merely develops what science uncovers. And the stuff science is uncovering these days is so huge that it's likely to change the way we look at the world, as well as how we interact with it.

At Berkeley, we sat with three of the brightest, most accomplished scientists in the world. To this day we wonder about two things:

• Why did we choose to talk to three world-class scientists about the meaning of life?
• Why did they agree to meet with us?

The answer to the first question is pretty easy. As we tried to think of what made the San Francisco Bay Area and Silicon Valley unique, we immediately thought about technology, and that eventually led us to the science. We knew we had to investigate the science community if we were going to look at technology as a metaphor for meaning. As for the second question, we still don't know the answer. We did get some phone numbers and e-mails from a friend in the public affairs office at Cal, but we didn't exactly have an open door. We basically cold called each of the scientists we interviewed, and all we told them was that we were searching for the meaning of life. Amazingly, all three agreed to meet with us.

MARC DAVIS: ENTHUSIASM FOR THE UNIVERSE

Our college transcripts are conspicuously void of any emphasis in science-related courses. Bruce majored in Theater Arts, and Stan was an English major, so each of us may have taken a mandatory course in biology, but that was it. (From time to time, people have commented on our degree of B.S., but we don't think they were referring to a bachelor of science degree.) So, walking on the Berkeley campus to meet with three of the world's top scientists was a bit intimidating for us.

Our fear and intimidation were dispelled when we walked into the office of Professor Marc Davis. We knew that Professor Davis was one of the world's foremost authorities and researchers on the large-scale universe and dark matter (although we weren't quite sure what that meant). Our preconceived notion had us expecting to find a mad scientist in a white lab coat who spoke with an Einstein accent and looked like Doc Brown from *Back to the Future*. What we found was a regular-looking guy named Marc dressed in Dockers and a polo shirt—not a lab coat in sight. And we immediately lost our reluctance to engage in a dialogue with him because his enthusiasm was infectious. We were so at ease that we asked him to explain the nature of his research to us. And he did it in a way that even we could understand.

"The subject of structure in the universe is something that developed over the last ten or twenty years. It's all intimately tied to theories of unification of the physical forces in the early universe and the nature of dark matter that dominates the universe—this mysterious stuff that astronomers talk about all of the time. We don't see it; it doesn't absorb or emit light; but it makes its presence felt by the gravitational pull it exerts on material. It is seen in galaxies, particularly outer regions of galaxies, and it had a large roll in the shaping of the universe and the clustering of the galaxies that we see around us. Much of my work has been involved in the study of this rather exotic stuff."

OK, so we didn't really understand it. But we were caught up in his excitement as he made grand gestures to describe the positioning of galaxy clusters. We asked about the purpose of his research.

"By mapping out the distribution of galaxies, then we can characterize the statistical properties of the galaxy clustering in space."

OK, but we still didn't get it. So he went on.

"With that information, then we can figure out why a galaxy distribution

WHERE YOU GONNA LIVE IF YOU'RE NOT IN A CYBER CAREER?

The high cost of housing in the Silicon Valley is tough enough for people pulling in those high-tech salaries. But it's even tougher for people working at jobs that don't pay according to the cyber wage scale. One study has found that high-tech wages may be as much as 220 percent higher than other private-sector wages. This disparity has made it almost impossible for people in nontechnical careers to live in the Silicon Valley.

The median price of a single-family home in the Bay Area is $385,000 (that means half the homes cost more and half the homes cost less). In Silicon Valley the median price jumps to $495,000. It is not uncommon for cottages in Palo Alto, about seventy years old and about nine hundred square feet, to sell for $600,000 (usually to be torn down so a more expensive home can be built on a lot that is 40' by 80'). If you can't afford to purchase a home (or you can't stand the idea of your "single-family" home consisting of two bedrooms and one bathroom in a part of town you wouldn't wish on your worst enemy), the only other alternative is to rent an apartment, but that's no walk in the park either.

We heard the story of a rookie officer in the California Highway Patrol who was assigned to Aptos in adjoining Santa Cruz County. His annual salary is $44,000. At that wage, he couldn't afford the $2,000 per month rent on a studio apartment. So he stayed in a hotel room at a cost of $1,096 per month. It wasn't home, but at least the maid service made his bed every day.

takes a particular form of filaments and voids. We want to analyze this information to see what it tells us about the parameters that govern our universe, and what it tells us about the constituents of our universe."

Now he had brought it down to earth and was talking about us (although it was the first time we had ever considered ourselves "constituents of the universe").

Professor Davis went on to say that all of this research is only possible because of the recent technological advancements.

"This is a subject that nobody thought to ask about until the technology made it possible to do the surveys to see what is out there. And it would be impossible to formulate the models without the very large computers that allowed us to simulate in great detail what is going on."

We were getting the impression that the universe was much more expansive than we had imagined. According to Professor Davis, the universe as we know it might be just one of many, and the others may be in dimensions that we can't comprehend.

"Our mathematical models, when combined with other ideas of what is happening in unified physics, leads us to suspect that the universe itself is eternal. Our universe is not eternal, but our particular universe is just a small piece of a larger megauniverse that can be thought of as a fluctuating bubble that existed in time before what is known as the Big Bang that produced our universe. This larger universe might have been in another dimension, and maybe many more dimensions. It could have existed indefinitely. Because it is in different dimensions, it can never be reached by us, so it is somewhat metaphysical."

It was time for Professor Davis to go to class. That was fortunate for us because the mental effort required to conceptualize metaphysical universes in other dimensions was about to burst the capillaries in our craniums.

We were still thinking about our place in an eternal universe as we walked across campus to our next appointment. We tried to apply our discussions with Marc Davis to the meaning of life and were struck by the irony of it all. It wasn't too long ago that sociologists had labeled college students as the "Me Generation" because of their self-centered attitudes. That generation, which supposedly felt that the universe revolved around them, is the same generation that produced the research and technological advancements that proved the enormity of the universe.

All of this talk about universes in other dimensions caused us to wonder if the meaning of life extended beyond ourselves.

CHARLES TOWNES: CONNECTING SCIENCE AND RELIGION

Before we met Charles Townes, we knew that he had won the Nobel Prize. We expected to see it sitting on his desk or hanging on his office wall (like a movie producer would display an Oscar). After all, this was the guy who developed the laser. His research and technological innovations have had broad application for science and society—from measuring the boundaries of outer space to the intricacies of eye surgery (not to mention the fun that twelve-year-old kids have putting red dots on the faces at the movies). But apparently scientists aren't quite as flamboyant as the Hollywood types, because we couldn't find the Nobel Prize medallion anywhere under or behind the stacks of research papers that cluttered his office.

When we were with Marc Davis, the term "religion" never came up (although we thought he might get there with his references to metaphysical universes in other dimensions, which caused us to think of heaven and hell). But Dr. Townes moved directly into that subject when we asked whether his research gave him any insights about the meaning of life. Instead of answering our direct question, he offered to give us a brief discourse of his opinion on the subject (to allow us to better frame our subsequent inquiries).

"Science is an attempt to understand the universe, to see what it is like and how it works. Science is exploration, discovery, and solving puzzles. Religion is an attempt to understand the meaning of the universe. If there is a meaning and purpose to it all, then it would clearly affect what the universe is really like. So studying what the universe is like ought to give some hints to what the meaning of life is all about."

We wondered whether interest in the relationship between science and religion was peculiar to him, or whether other scientists were equally interested in a correlation between their research and the meaning of it all. Dr. Townes said that all sciences, especially the physical sciences, are digging into the meaning of life.

"Particularly in physics and astronomy, scientists have been getting into more and more fundamental questions that relate to meaning. As we dig into these areas, most physical scientists have become impressed with how special our universe is, and how special our Earth is. Somehow everything happened to turn out just right. The laws of physics have to be exactly a certain way in order for the stars to exist, the earth to exist, and for life to exist. Without the precision and the matching that is required, then none of this could have happened. This leads many scientists to say that, clearly, there has to be some intelligent planning—some mind and intelligence—behind it all. Even if they don't want to talk about God, they acknowledge that there is something here that has done all of this."

What he was saying made it sound like there was a causal connection between science and religion—that the two weren't mutually exclusive.

"In the past that might have been the case, but not any longer. Now the feeling of mutual exclusivity has died out. With scientific research, particularly in the physical sciences, people aren't so hesitant to talk about religion and meaning. A good number of scientists are religious. It is my personal view that those two—science and religion—must be related. When we understand them both well enough, then it is my guess that they will both eventually come together."

This was no cold-hearted, emotionless, analytical cyborg that sat before us. Dr. Townes had obviously grappled with the ramifications of meaning behind all of his scientific research.

"My personal meaning comes, in part, from finding out how science works and developing human understanding and mental capacity. It is very stimulating to understand something better or see something new that hasn't been recognized before. The progress of science and technology is part of the purpose and meaning of life."

> "Western civilization, it seems to me, stands by two great heritages.
>
> One is the scientific spirit of adventure—the adventure into the unknown, an unknown that must be recognized as unknown in order to be explored, the demand that the unanswerable mysteries of the universe remain unanswered, the attitude that all is uncertain. To summarize it: humility of the intellect.
>
> The other great heritage is Christian ethics—the basis of action on love, the brotherhood of all men, the value of the individual, the humility of the spirit."
>
> —Richard Feynman, *The Meaning of It All*

But he shifted from the technical to the intimate when he mentioned the other part of life where he finds meaning.

"I think meaning also has a lot to do with human relationships. We need love and we need association and interaction with others. That is a very important part of the purpose and meaning of life."

GEORGE SMOOT:
MARVELING AT THE UNIVERSE AND ITS MEANING

It was appropriate and rather symbolic that our last interview of the day at UC Berkeley took us to the very top of the campus to the Lawrence Berkeley National Laboratory, where scientific research of the highest order takes place on a daily basis. To give you an idea of just how high this research goes, our appointment was with the man who has literally peered into the very beginning of the universe. On April 24, 1992, a team of astrophysicists let by George Smoot announced that the Cosmic Background Explorer (COBE) satellite had measured the ripples in the cosmic background radiation. In Bruce & Stan terms, that means that Dr. Smoot and his team had detected the heat from the first creation event, otherwise known as the Big Bang. Stephen Hawking called it "the discovery of the century, if not of all time."

Science had speculated about the Big Bang creation event for some time, but no one had ever demonstrated it. Until Dr. Smoot came along. And we were about to sit down with him and talk about the meaning of life. When we finally found Dr. Smoot's office, we were surprised to find him alone, sitting in the corner of his office in front of three large computer screens. There was scientific paraphernalia everywhere, along with a white board containing complex scientific formulas (it was like a scene from a movie). George welcomed us in and talked warmly and openly about the stuff he does and the meaning it has.

In the corner opposite his desk was a strange contraption that looked like it belonged in space. He noticed us gazing at it and said, "That's a piece of the COBE satellite, or at least the prototype. Another piece is in the Smithsonian." We stared at it a while longer until Dr. Smoot invited us to sit down for what would be a thirty-minute interview. Here are the highlights.

Bruce & Stan: Why is it so important that we know the universe had a beginning?

George Smoot: For the first time we have a consistent story about how the universe was created and can explain the stages from a teeny fraction of a second. It's a story that most of humankind will take forward as their story. Different cultures have always had different stories about origins and the end of the world and how their particular culture fits into that. We're the first generation to have an actual story that's plausible and testable as to how the universe came from extremely early times to the present.

B&S: You've literally peered into the beginning of the universe. What meaning has that brought to your life?

GS: I had the privilege of spending a lot of my time to make those measurements as they were coming and to understand them before other people did. I have had time to reflect on what it means. The implications are big, but it's not clear what the impact will be. If your idea of God is that he is an entity in terms of a certain locality, well, this is an awfully big universe, so if there's a God, then he has to be infinite and he has to be everywhere all the time.

I look at it and I just marvel at two aspects. First, that the universe is understandable. You can test it and probe it. You can have a good understanding of what could have been very messy and difficult to understand. Second, how beautifully it all fits together. It's beautiful in an abstract sense rather than a personal sense. In other words, you don't get the idea that the universe is your mother. You get the idea that the universe is this wonderful stage full of raw materials and activities and as a person, you're incidental. It's up to you to make your way in the universe, and to be amazed by it.

B&S: Are you saying that the meaning of life is connected to a design and purpose for the universe and for our lives?

GS: It's good to ask these frontier questions. I've been thinking about this lately. A large part of the meaning of life has to do with the individual. People have to make their own meaning of life. I don't subscribe to the idea that there was a design and purpose to life, and that everyone is striving to find it. On the other hand, there is clearly a lot to be gained in life by seeing its richness and using your abilities to move forward ethically and culturally. There's a lot more to life than mere existence.

It's so clear and true, how can anybody doubt it? And yet people ask, is this all there is, just existence? That's because some people get up in the morning, put on their shoes, go to work, come home, and then go to bed because they're tired and have to get up tomorrow and do it over again. Fortunately, most people don't live that way these days. Our economy, social structure, and our science and technology have developed to where most people can have an extra richness to life.

We have books and flowers and the beauty of the sunset. I think it's so obvious that there's more to life than existence. There's meaning and purpose as well.

As we left Dr. Smoot's office, we paused for a moment on the steps outside the Lawrence Berkeley Lab. The entire Bay Area was spread out before us like a painting. The sky above seemed so vast and infinite, while the people below seemed so small and insignificant.

SOMETHING BIGGER THAN YOU

Feeling insignificant isn't all that bad. You really ought to try it sometime. If you're like we are, you've probably spent most of your life trying to feel significant. But that can be a rather exhausting experience. There's all that studying and positioning and schmoozing and achieving and always trying to be at the right place at the right time. Sometimes it feels good just to sit back, relax, and realize that there's a universe—and things in the universe, and a God bigger than the universe—at work on a very grand scale. When you get to that point—and believe us, we were there when we walked down that hill at Berkeley—your own question of purpose and meaning becomes very simple. You stop asking, "What can I do that's never been done before?" and you start asking, "How can I get involved in something bigger than I am?"

We directed our rental car across the Bay Bridge, through San Francisco, and south along Highway 101 to Palo Alto. We had been to UC Berkeley to get the perspective of science, and now it was time to visit Stanford

University for the technology slant. Stanford is known as the leading technology incubator in the world. Every year its graduates—from engineers to MBAs to entrepreneurs—have a huge impact on the high-tech world. Stanford grads William Hewlett and David Packard pioneered the industry when they started their company in 1939. Since then some of the most visible and successful high-tech companies in the world have been founded by

TRODDING THE PATHS OF THE QUAD

The Bay Area is home to many colleges and universities. On the private side, there is Santa Clara University, University of San Francisco, and St. Mary's College, just to name just a few. On the public side, there is Cal State University at Hayward, San Jose State University, and San Francisco State University. But as fine as these institutions are, there are two other institutions that garner all of the academic attention and straddle the Bay like twin ivory towers.

One of these academic heavyweights is on the west side of the Bay in Palo Alto. Most people know it as Stanford, but it is really "the Leland Stanford Junior University." Don't be confused. It is not a Junior University (like a two-year junior college) that was established by Leland Stanford. No, it is a full-fledged university that was founded by Leland Stanford, Jr.

In the East Bay, there is the University of California at Berkeley. This is the university that was famous for radicals and protests in the '60s and '70s and early '80s. Things quieted down after that, and by the late '80s its primary notoriety was "the naked guy" that used to walk around campus. (After years of allowing protests that complained about the shortcomings of society, apparently the authorities couldn't arrest a guy who was flaunting his.) By the 1990s, the protests were over, the naked guy was draped, and UC Berkeley had established itself as one of the premier scientific research institutes in the world.

We learned something else about Berkeley, but we learned it by reading a license plate frame on a car we saw parked in the faculty lot on the Stanford campus. It said

"YOU CAN ALWAYS TELL A BERKELEY GRAD,
BUT YOU CAN'T TELL HIM MUCH."

Stanford alum: Netscape, Sun Microsystems, Silicon Graphics, Cisco, Excite, and Yahoo! are a few examples.

We tracked down two recent graduates of Stanford's engineering school to get a meaning-of-life perspective on technology. Brian Moore and Todd Dickson were friends at Stanford, and both ended up working for the same company in Palo Alto, a rather small firm that specializes in designing and manufacturing micromedical devices used in heart surgery. We asked Brian and Todd if they were influenced by the high-tech frenzy and the lure of riches when they were undergraduates.

"Some of the people on the forefront of the dotcom hype were in our class. The guys who started Yahoo! [Jerry Yang and David Filo] were around, although we didn't know them personally. There has always been a spirit of innovation at Stanford, but this latest euphoria based on making money on electrons rather than actual products has burst for all practical purposes."

We detected a note of satisfaction when they said this. So we asked the next logical question: "What kind of meaning does it give you to know that you are working on a product that actually saves lives instead of a service that allows us to order dog food on-line?"

"We're kind of arrogant about that," they both agreed, and then they laughed. Then Todd gave us his story. "I have always had an entrepreneurial bent, but when I finally became skilled in engineering, I decided to work on actual products. My background is medicine—my father is a doctor—but I didn't want to follow in his footsteps. I wanted to do something that hadn't been done before. Then, as I matured, I realized that I didn't have to be the first of the first of the first. I simply needed to get involved with something meaningful. So I joined this company because I was excited about saving lives and building something that was a net plus."

We asked Todd what he meant by that (we're not exactly hip to the high-tech lingo).

"In the past this valley was devoted primarily to manufacturing weapons and products that effectively destroy lives, or at least didn't improve them in any way. People made money on that, so there was a net profit. Now this Valley is more and more becoming involved in things that are a net plus. You can make a profit, but your products can also benefit people. It's very fulfilling to be involved in things that save lives rather than destroy them. That is very compelling to me."

Todd and Brian showed us the products they design. They are tubular structures called stents that are inserted into arteries and other body tubes to prevent them from becoming blocked by disease. Todd's own father had a heart attack a few years ago and was restored to health with the help of a stent, so the impact of what Todd is involved with hit very close to home. We couldn't help but ask Todd about his own mortality. What if he had a brush with death, and then was granted three more quality years to live?

"I would throw my weight into what I see as the potential of this valley. The potential for this area to affect the rest of the world is much greater than what is happening now, so I would dedicate myself to that. This valley should be an asset for the world, not just a piggy bank. We have the universities and the think tanks. There is a community of educated, forward-looking, change-oriented, motivated, driven people who have the potential to effect the rest of the world for good."

We wondered if that would be ultimately meaningful.

"That's the big question. My view is that this generation has given up on significance in order to enjoy life. They don't just want to make more money, if it means selling out to the company. They want to do what they want when they want. My hope is that there are still enough people out there who are willing to respond to the idea that they can have a significant life."

OK, so how do you define significance?

"In my view significance is achieved by doing two things. First, you need to know what your gifts are or could be, and then work to develop them. Second, you need to find out what is bigger than you, and then get involved in it. Rather than saying, 'I can be the center of a big company,' take the view that something big is already happening, then get on board with that.

"Figure out how your gifts create a space for you to be involved."

SOUL OF THE CITY

We felt a kinship with the Silicon Valley. It, too, seemed to be searching for the meaning of life.

So much has happened so rapidly in the Silicon Valley. At times the area seems to be very comfortable and confident in its role as a world scientific and technological leader, and other times it seems to be reeling from all of it (such as when the bottom drops out of the NASDAQ and the scramble is on to pull out of a tech tailspin). From what we could see, the Valley is still in the process of letting the dust settle so it can get its bearings. It's trying to find its own distinctive perspective on life.

The Silicon Valley's unique combination of science, technology, and prosperity has caused the residents to confront meaning-of-life issues perhaps more than any other city we visited. While it seems that the perspectives are still in the formative stages, we detected three dominant philosophies.

The meaning of life may be bigger than life as we know it. You can't grapple with the scientific research on the origin and expanse of the universe without wondering if there is much more out there than we realize. The cosmologists (that would be those scientists that study the cosmos, not the beauty-school graduates) and the astrophysicists in academic institutions and private research firms throughout the Bay Area have sensitized this region to dimensions beyond planet Earth. Each successive scientific finding—whether through the telescopes of astronomers searching the farthest reaches of the universe or through the microscopes of molecular biologists searching for genetic clues—strengthens the conclusion that the structures of the universe were intelligently designed. Design is dictated by purpose. Purpose is derived from meaning.

The meaning of life goes beyond yourself. The avarice for dotcom wealth and the yearning for IPO profits have subsided a bit. That doesn't mean that the techies have slacked off. They continue to work hard (sixty to eighty hours a week is not uncommon), but their motivation is not solely a monetary one. There seems to be a legitimate and sincere desire to develop technology that has a beneficial purpose. The Silicon Valley is not a "me" culture. It is outward and other directed. Meaning has been found in producing results that are significant for society.

The meaning of life entails some attainment of balance in life. There is no shortage of stories in the *San Jose Mercury News* about high-tech execs who are pulling the plug—figuratively and literally. Family life seems to be the reason. One example is Ray Lane who resigned the No. 2 post at Oracle to get his life in balance and reconnect with his family. "Ultimately, time is the most important asset," Lane said. "Not money. Not fame. It's time, and it's how you utilize that time. My youngest daughter said I didn't spend enough time with her. And back then I'd say, 'It's not the quantity of time. It's the quality of time.' I can now see how stupid that was."

Another example is young executive Alay Desai, the chief technology offi-cer at Stario.com, who has no electronic gadgets in his home except a used TV. "I don't need all those laptops and cell phones and Palm Pilots. Technology is a tool to make things, to create something of lasting value. It's not meant to control my life. I won't let it enslave me." Whether the enslave-ment is the high-tech career or the technology itself, many of the inhabitants of Silicon Valley eschew it for the sake of realizing deeper meaning in life.

As we departed from Silicon Valley, these were our impressions about the meaning of life. Stan feverishly typed up our notes on our reliable Dell lap-top while Bruce drove our semireliable rental car south on Highway 101. We were leaving Northern California on our way to Southern California, with a slight detour over to Highway 99 that runs down the center of the state so we could route our search through Fresno. We didn't plan on interviewing anyone in Fresno, but we wanted to look at the "Welcome to Fresno" sign along the highway. There was a rumor that it was emblazoned with the city's motto: "We live here so you don't have to."

departure
08942

NEXT STOP: HOLLYWOOD

10

arrival mileage

0 9 4 4 3

HOLLYWOOD:
Making Life Entertaining

Before we get into this chapter, we have a confession to make. We'd like to make a movie or have our own half-hour prime-time sitcom, and we're hoping you can help us out. The way we figure it, there's always been room in the movies or on television for a couple of crazy characters who are constantly getting themselves into and out of trouble. There has been Stan & Ollie, Martin & Lewis, Ricky & Lucy, Andy & Barney. Why not Bruce & Stan? We're as lovable as any of those comedy couples. All we need is a chance. Why don't we do lunch at Spago's? What do you say? Let's sync our Palm Pilots and set it up. Deal? No? You're busy for the next few years? C'mon, can't you give a couple of talented guys a break? Excuse us, but was that really called for? Oh, yeah? Well, see if we ever ask you about the meaning of life!

*　　*　　*

OK, so maybe we got a little carried away, but that's what happens when you go to Hollywood. Whether you're there for business or pleasure, something very strange happens the minute you come under the spell of this very unusual town. No matter what you do in your real life, you start getting these illusions about making it in Hollywood. You could be a very professional, hard-working person back in Omaha, but as soon as you get to Hollywood, you start dreaming about becoming some sort of star. That image of you on TV or the silver screen is so real you can taste it.

What is it about Hollywood that does this to people? Few places evoke such emotion. No other city in the world has such a mystique. In fact, Hollywood isn't a city at all, but rather an unincorporated district in the northwestern part of the city of Los Angeles. Maybe that's symbolic of what Hollywood really is. More than a place, Hollywood is a symbol for our dreams and desires.

Los Angeles CityFacts

FOUNDED: 1781
CITY POPULATION: 3,597,556
METRO AREA: 15 million plus
NICKNAMES: City of Angels, Tinsel Town
BUT WE CALL IT: LaLa Land
KNOWN FOR: Motion picture and television industries, earthquakes, riots, freeways
FAMOUS NATIVES: Jodie Foster, Dustin Hoffman, Marilyn Monroe, Adlai Stevenson, Darryl Strawberry

These are the kinds of things we were thinking about as we climbed over the Tehachapi Mountains and descended into the Los Angeles basin. Honestly, we had no illusions about making it in Tinsel Town, but we have to admit to having a few fantasies about getting into the film or television business. Who hasn't? As a culture, we're surrounded by the media every day: We watch television, listen to the radio, go to the movies, log onto the Internet, buy CDs, and rent videos and DVDs.

Why are we so hungry for all this creative input? We think it has something to do with the age-old fascination with drama and stories. From the time of the early Greek theater to the flowering of the Elizabethan stage to the dawning of *Star Wars,* human beings around the globe have been captivated by a good story. The greatest communicators have always been the best storytellers: Moses, Homer (the Greek poet, not Simpson), Jesus, Chaucer, Shakespeare, and Lucas. Whether these geniuses were communicating from a hillside, a stage, or a movie screen, their stories have stirred the passions of untold millions.

Ultimately it's the story—whether truth or fiction, tragedy or comedy—that connects people with the deeper issues of life. The way we look at it, stories give us insights and access to the meaning of life. At least that's what we found when we went to Hollywood. See if you don't agree.

THAT'S ENTERTAINMENT!

Sometimes we had to spend several days in a city before we could find its connection to our search. As it turned out, the personality or characteristics of each city fit into a definable theme for meaning in life, but sometimes we had to look hard to find it. Not so in Hollywood. There the connection was obvious. It couldn't be anything other than entertainment. After all, Hollywood is the entertainment capital of the world. But don't take our word for it. Just go to Hollywood and talk to the myriad of aspiring actors, directors, and screenwriters about it when they ask you if you want to supersize your order of burger and fries.

Entertainment is the way people tell stories. It's always been that way, but it never seems more true than today, in the technology-laden twenty-first century. Someone comes up with an idea, which leads to a script, which leads to a production involving directors, actors, technicians, special-effects specialists, and editors—the list goes on. Eventually the story comes out in a movie or gets put on television, and hopefully people watch it. First and foremost the story has to be entertaining, or people won't watch it. That's the bottom line in Hollywood. If it's not entertaining, it's not successful.

Everything is out in the open in Hollywood. We aren't referring to alfresco restaurants and cafés (although they are ubiquitous). We mean that everything about Hollywood is in your face. The city's unofficial slogan must be: "If you've got it, flaunt it." (And if you don't have it, then there are two other slogans that apply: (a) "Fake it till you make it," or (b) "A good plastic surgeon can give you whatever God didn't.")

Nothing is flaunted more in Hollywood than the city's connection to the entertainment industry. There are those bronze stars in the sidewalk along Hollywood Boulevard, many of which commemorate the careers of a bunch of dead people who no one remembers from the early days of radio, television, and movies. Then there are the grand and historic movie studios that serve as constant reminders to Hollywood's Golden Era: RKO, MGM, Warner Brothers, Columbia Pictures, and Twentieth Century Fox. Of course, with consolidation and foreign investors, there have been ignominious transitions, such as when Columbia was bought by Paramount, which in turn was acquired by Sony. But despite changes in the industry, Hollywood remains synonymous with the movies. Hollywood won't let us forget its glorious past because it wants to preserve its place at the front of the entertainment line.

No city could threaten to usurp Hollywood's claim as the entertainment capital. Within commuting distance is the largest pool of talent (on both sides of the camera) that exists in the world. If you want to be in show business, you start in Hollywood. This principle applies to the wannabe stars, but it also applies to the heavyweights. When Spielberg, Katzenberg, and Geffen started DreamWorks, they didn't look for office space in Denver.

The HOLLYWOOD Sign

Even the famed Hollywood sign has a story. It was first constructed on a rugged hillside in 1923 as an advertisement for a real estate development called "Hollywoodland" (the "land" was removed in 1945). After deteriorating badly, the sign was revitalized in the 1970s, thanks to private donations. The best view of the fifty-foot tall, 450-foot wide, 450,000-pound sign is from Beachwood Drive just north of Hollywood Boulevard.

Yes, as we drove into town and saw the famous HOLLYWOOD sign on the hill, we immediately knew that we'd be thinking about the ways entertainment brings meaning to life. Entertainment was destined to be our theme for this city. It was in the stars.

WHAT'S ENTERTAINMENT?

We knew we were going to consider the meaning of life in the context of entertainment. But we got a slow start because it took us a few days to absorb the meaning of entertainment. That single word, entertainment, can be defined to mean something as simplistic as amusement. But that one-dimensional definition is not applicable in Hollywood. Hollywood is entertainment, and it is much more than mere amusement. Entertainment in Hollywood is a convoluted mixture of culture, business, and lifestyle. It apparently involves a four-stage process that is sort of like a food chain—it requires that you eat or be eaten:

Stage 1: Self-Promotion. You have to make sure that you get noticed in this town. You are nobody if they don't know who you are. The only way you are going to get discovered is to stand out from the crowd. You gotta sell yourself, baby.

Stage 2: Celebrity Status. If you have excelled at self-promotion, then you are on your way to celebrity status. If you have both celebrity and talent, then you can progress to the next stage (see below). But if you lack ability, you won't rise any higher than mere celebrity. You'll be relegated to supermarket tabloid headlines and game shows like Hollywood Squares. ("I'll take Gary Coleman for the block.") Many sagging celebrities resort to outlandish fashions to garner attention. This isn't difficult for most of them because they have lots of money and they believe that it confers taste and class, but it doesn't (as evidenced by the outfits worn to any awards show).

Stage 3: The Buzz. Hollywood operates on buzz. We learned that buzz is the energy, excitement, and a sense of expectancy that the right person can bring to a project. A certain level of talent is required to reach this stage, but talent alone is not enough. There's also got to be some star quality about the person. Mere talent isn't as important as buzz-ability because the publicity surrounding people is more important than the quality of their work. (Note to readers: Don't mistake hype for buzz. Hype is manufactured and phony. Buzz is generated naturally from the anticipation about a project. Hype is out. Buzz is in. Got it? Good. Now you're hip to hype.)

Stage 4: Influence. There are a select few in Hollywood who wield tremendous influence in the entertainment business. There are two types of people at Stage 4. There are the creative types: These are the people who have tremendous talent but have also excelled at stages 1, 2, and 3. (Talent alone doesn't get you squat without those other stages.) And there are those who are the successful and shrewd business types: Usually these are studio executives. (A high-level corporate position at a studio doesn't automatically confer Stage 4 status. As one insider told us, "There have always been morons in high places.") Whether they get there by talent or business acumen, the people at Stage 4 are in a position to control the projects in Hollywood.

Sociologists recognize that Hollywood has a tremendous and disproportionate power to shape our culture. You might think that the celebrities at Stage 2 make this happen. Well, they might set fashion trends, but they really don't affect our culture, at least not in significant ways. After the studio system was established in Hollywood, the culture shaping was in the hands of those who had made it to Stage 4, and that's pretty much been the way it's been—until recently. The times and traditions are changing in Hollywood.

THE INFLUENCE OF ENTERTAINMENT

We discovered that there is a grass-roots level of people in Hollywood who are passionate about using entertainment to influence the culture. These aren't the celebrities, and they aren't the powerful Stage 4 types. They are the behind-the-sceners.

In much the same way that *The Blair Witch Project* challenged the traditional studios, there are many professionals in Hollywood who refuse to leave culture shaping to the Stage 4 power brokers. They have something they want to say to society, and they want to use television, movies, and music as their way to communicate. We talked with several members of this revolution, and we were captivated by their passion to influence their culture.

HOLLYWOOD AND LOS ANGELES

Although it is the most famous part of Los Angeles, Hollywood is just one part of this sprawling megalopolis. Los Angeles is the largest and most populated consolidated metropolitan statistical area in the country. It covers 460 square miles and includes eighty incorporated cities connected by a maze of freeways unique in the world. You can see Hollywood from the 101 Freeway (appropriately named the Hollywood Freeway), but to experience Hollywood, you have to take the surface streets, such as Melrose, Santa Monica, Sunset, or Hollywood Boulevards.

J. A. C. REDFORD: ATTUNED TO HOLLYWOOD

J. A. C. Redford is a composer. He is classically trained, and his orchestrations reflect it. He has written the musical scores for numerous films, television shows, and miniseries. We met with J. A. C. in a typical Southern California restaurant (lots of salad and vegetables; no beef). Between bites of tofu, sprouts, and pasta, we listened as he gave us his keen insights about Hollywood.

Because J. A. C. works behind the scenes, far from the spotlight and the paparazzi, he has gained an objective perspective about both the good and bad aspects of Hollywood and the entertainment business. We began our interview by asking about current films. J. A. C.'s response surprised us a bit.

"A lot is happening now in Hollywood, and there are a lot of films being made, but creative people are feeling stifled. This is not a good time for creativity in movies. There is too much formula. Some of the most creative work being done now is found in the foreign films. They figure that Hollywood has got the formula covered, so they try to do something innovative."

We followed up with a question about what he views as the creative challenges to the composer of a film score.

"I know that the audience will come into the theater careworn and burdened with their personal problems. I want the worry to drift off their faces as they become engaged with my music and the story of the film. I love it when the director treats the composer as a creative partner and gives the composer enough freedom to experiment. That's when I have the chance to surprise him with something he didn't plan in advance."

All of this talk about composition was fascinating, but he hadn't yet mentioned the names of any movie stars. We had been watching the Hollywood gossip TV shows and reading *People* and *Entertainment* magazines in preparation for our visit to Hollywood. We were ready to hear a little inside dirt about the stars, so Stan blurted out, "What are the movie stars really like?" J. A. C. still didn't drop any names, but he did give us an interesting behind-the-camera perspective.

"Well, let me say this first: Stan, you have a piece of spinach leaf stuck between your teeth. Now, let me answer your question. The media focuses in on a few artists, and then society makes them our heroes. When we give them that elevated status, we begin to think that they can teach us something about life. But they are hurting people just like the rest of us. Hero worship has its rewards for the hero, but those rewards are transitory. More than anybody, they realize that there is no lasting sense of significance just because they are given the red-carpet treatment. Everything they do, in their professional work and their personal life, is the subject of scrutiny and judgment. They read the raves about their work, then they go back to their trailers and worry about whether they can repeat the performance. At any given moment, many stars are either loathing themselves or thinking that they are better than everyone else is. We should pity these people, not worship them."

Our next question was a no-brainer: "If fame doesn't bring real meaning to life in Hollywood, then what does?"

"You can find significance in doing a good job. It is easy to identify the people who realize this. You hear them talking more about their work than themselves. Take Stephen Sondheim for example. He never talks about himself; he always talks about his craft. These people have realized a sense of satisfaction."

J. A. C. quickly explained that doing a good job should not be confused with having a good job. "Those who haven't yet realized a sense of satisfaction in the quality of their work are always looking for 'a good job.' That term is usually equated with a job or project that is unhealthy for a balanced life; a job that that will bring lots of fame but requires you to abandon your family in the process."

We left our meeting with J. A. C. a little better equipped for the rest of our interviews in Hollywood. We had learned important lessons about looking past the glitter of celebrities and about discretely using a toothpick.

THE CATHEDRAL OF THE NEW MILLENNIUM

Douglas Briggs, the director of the Los Angeles Film Studies Center, has some very interesting opinions about the place and importance of movies in our culture. According to Briggs, the cathedral of the present generation is the cineplex (those huge structures that contain twenty or more movie theaters within a complex and usually include restaurants and shops).

Through the 1970s, the church played a central role in American culture. It was the place where people gathered and shared their beliefs and emotions with each other. It was a place that united individual families, and communities, and the nation in shared views and values. But in the last two decades, the cineplex has usurped the role of the church. Now people gather and socialize there. More significantly, the values that are adopted by our culture are those proclaimed on the screen.

While society used to find its principles in the Bible, now it looks to the entertainment industry for truth. Whether it is via films, television, cable, Internet, magazines, or music, the entertainment industry provides the content that Americans absorb as their source of guidance.

MICHAEL GONZALES: THE PROFESSOR

Dr. Michael Gonzales is an associate professor in the Radio-Television-Film department of Biola University in Los Angeles. He is also an adjunct professor at the USC School of Film and Television. In addition to teaching full-time, Michael is a successful screenwriter. We interviewed Michael in his office at Biola.

Bruce & Stan: A lot of the students you teach are Christians. Why do you encourage Christians to go into the entertainment industry?

Michael Gonzales: Hollywood is a mission field, and it's been long neglected as that. I tell my students to go out there and make a difference. And then I give them some armor so they can survive.

B&S: What kind of armor?

MG: It has to do with who they are and who God is. I tell my students two things. First, walk in humility. That takes more than being humble. It's a process to get to that place. I encourage them to be grateful and to give themselves to God. Second, keep your antennae up and find that frequency where God is at.

B&S: In this mission field, do you express yourself more through the work you do or through the relationships you build?

MG: I think it's both. The relationships come first, because if you write a script, you won't be able to put John 3:16 in there. It's just not going to happen. But you can make a difference in terms of how you conduct yourself.

B&S: Talk about entertainment. When is entertainment meaningful?

MG: Sometimes it can just be entertainment and levity from the daily grind. It doesn't have to have a plus or minus sign. In a sense, entertainment is a neutral commodity. But it is a commodity in which people can make a living, so it's perfectly reasonable for a Christian to seek entertainment as a career goal in order to make a difference while holding a job. I've been successful in the film business, but I've learned that it's not about money. For me it's people. I invest myself in people, and I've learned to trust God to put food on the table.

B&S: But isn't it really hard to maintain your Christian values in the film business?

MG: It's easier to be a Christian in the industry now than ever, because the support systems are out there for actors, writers, directors, and technical people. If you're serious about being in the business as a Christian, you need to stay close to an accountability group of people who are doing what you're doing, and you'll survive. Little by little everybody moves up the ladder. I tell my film students that they are part of the cultural elite. The rest of the world looks to what they are going to produce. The opportunities are wide open to those who want to be directors and writers. There are positions available for those who are willing to work and build relationships. And it doesn't much matter that you went to the USC Film School. What people want to know is, "Are you real?" If you're real and there's integrity in your work, people will pay attention.

SCOTT DERRICKSON: THE DIRECTOR

Scott Derrickson is living the American dream, that is if your dream is to have a three-picture deal with a major Hollywood studio to write and direct your own films—and you haven't even hit thirty yet. We immediately liked Scott for two reasons. First, he is a deep thinker and a thinking Christian (a rarity in Hollywood); and two, he has a writing partner. Hey, he's a guy after our own heart. We had a heart-to-heart talk with Scott in the Hamburger Hamlet directly across the street from the famous Mann's Chinese Theater on Hollywood Boulevard.

We started by asking Scott the question we asked everybody on our cross-country tour: Where do you find your meaning in life?

"I am a person who is obsessed with the subject of meaning. I find ultimate meaning for myself in Scripture: 'What does the Lord require of you but to do justice, to love mercy, and to walk humbly with your God' [Micah 6:8]. I find meaning in everything if I am seeing life correctly. My favorite book in Scripture is Ecclesiastes. It's the book of meaning. What you learn is that meaning cannot be found by honest seekers in the form they desire to find it, mainly because there is a certain mystery to meaning. So Ecclesiastes ultimately says, go enjoy your life, enjoy your work, try to behave appropriately, and don't be overrighteous. In the end, fear God and keep his commandments. Do that, and you're free to enjoy everything else."

"What about Hollywood," we asked Scott. "Do many people find meaning here?"

"Hollywood is a menagerie of creatures running around seeking meaning in the wrong places. Those places where people look are pretty predictable—beauty, youth, money, fame—but the great sin of Hollywood isn't the craving for any of that. The great sin is idolatry, in that making the deal or getting the role become god. People are frantically trying to either attain their idols or maintain them. It's difficult for anybody who wants to really pursue what is ultimately meaningful to not participate in that. As a Christian you have to withdraw somehow to remind yourself that those things are not that important."

OK, we get the withdrawal thing. But we wondered if it's possible for a Christian to make films and bring a Christian worldview into the picture (in a manner of speaking). Is that a good way to affect the culture?

"Anybody who approaches the creative process with that sort of agenda is destined to thwart good creativity. You end up writing propaganda and not something that's going to be irresistible. Some of my favorite films are about themes I am diametrically opposed to, but they are so well done with such honesty and truthfulness that you can't help but be absorbed in them and find tremendous value. Christians have been guilty of not doing that."

Scott had given us an entirely different perspective than we were expecting. Here was a young man who believes that you can't start with an agenda to impact the culture. If you do, you take yourself outside the creative process. But if you maintain that process and the integrity of your craft, the truth will emerge, and the culture will be impacted.

FRED JUDKINS: THE CRAFTSMAN

After graduating with a degree in Television and Radio from San Diego State University, Fred Judkins entered the studio system as a sound editor. In his twenty-five-year career, he has prepped sound tracks for thousands of hours of television and done around a hundred feature films. We caught up with Fred on the Sony Pictures Studio lot, where he works for Steve and Judee Flick's Creative Café, the only studio in town with two Oscars for sound effects. Fred is one of the most respected sound editors in the business (he was working on Billy Bob Thornton's *All the Pretty Horses* starring Matt Damon when we met with him). But don't let his credentials fool you. Fred is even goofier than we are, which is why we like him so much.

Our interview with Fred was so convoluted that we can't really put it in a typical Q & A format. So we're just going to let Fred spout off in a kind of stream of consciousness style. We asked Fred about the people he works with—his peers, the actors, the studio heads—and we asked him about how Hollywood and the meaning of life go together.

> Most people who work in Hollywood at my level, which is at the craftsman level, are looking for a happy, safe, fulfilling life. The actors are

here to make money and become famous. You don't go to Hollywood to meet deep thinkers. You go to Hollywood to make a lot of money and get a lot of power for yourself.

Everybody seems to be so nutty over people who become famous. That doesn't make you any happier. If just makes you more famous. It's no secret that the Hollywood establishment is notoriously shallow. They're not giving any answers to anybody who's looking for answers. They're creating problems that seem very big and very noisy.

For me the whole battle is the battle for the brain and for ideas. For Christians, if you're going to aim for any industry, regardless of what it is, you've got to aim your sights for where you can be heard. In Hollywood, it's the war of ideas. At the same time, this is a business of relationships. As a Christian, I can be loving to the people I work with, I can be honest, I can have integrity, and I can treat them the way I want to be treated. This is true of Christians in any profession. People first want to know if you love them and care for them, before they know how good you are.

If I had the ability to aim higher than where I am, I would aim higher. If God gifted me with the talents to be a producer, or to own a newspaper, or to run CNN, or to go on-line and create something that's never been done before to influence people for Christ, then I would do that. Shoot as high as you possibly can. If you think you are at a certain level, aim higher, because God is going to take you to some place that you've never even thought about.

For me, meaning comes at the beginning of each day, because as soon as I wake up I commit the day to the Lord. I ask Jesus Christ to bless the day, keep me safe, keep my family safe, and help me to show his love wherever I go. That's my goal every day.

MICHAEL WARREN: THE PRODUCER

Michael Warren is one of the most successful television producers in Hollywood. Since 1973 Michael has been a writer and producer for some of the best-known family sitcoms in television history, including *Happy Days, Perfect Strangers,* and *Family Matters.* All told he has produced more than seven hundred episodes of prime-time television. We caught up with Michael in his office suite on the Warner Brothers Studio lot.

Bruce & Stan: What are people looking for in Hollywood?

Michael Warren: Most people I know who work in television want to do a product they can be proud of. They want to be able to go home at night and say, "I work on *West Wing,*" or "I work on a hit show that wins Emmys," or whatever their criteria for success is. As a Christian, that's never been very interesting to me. What I like is the process of making television shows and working with people.

B&S: Hollywood isn't the family-friendliest place on the planet. Has it been difficult being known as the family guy in television circles?

You Are What You Drive

The automobile (or truck or SUV or Humvee) is the symbol of mobile status in Hollywood and Los Angeles. Unless you have your own set of wheels, you won't get anywhere in Southern California, and unless your wheels make a statement, you won't get anywhere in Hollywood. We knew this, of course, which is why we tried very hard to trade in our heap of a rental car for something more suited to a couple of happening guys like us. We paid a visit to the Exotic Car Rental Agency in Beverly Hills and found the following choices available to us (prices are for a one-day rental):

Acura NSX	$425
Porsche 996 Cabriolet	$525
Dodge Viper	$599
Mercedes CL 500	$625
Ferrari F355 Spider	$990

We were ready to sign up for the Ferrari when we noticed in the contract that there was a two-day minimum on the rental, so we walked out (also, we noticed that the manager had called the Beverly Hills Cops when our car started leaking oil).

MW: The challenge is always finding people who are willing to come along with you on that journey. This may sound ridiculous, but it's true. So many people don't want to do a family show because they can't go to a Hollywood party and say they work on *Family Matters.* They'd much rather say they wrote last week's *Seinfeld.* That's the way you get recognition in this community.

B&S: What advice would you give to someone who wants to get into the entertainment industry?

MW: First, get a very broad, high-quality liberal arts education. You have to be a literate person because you're constantly communicating with people through letters, memos, and e-mails. The mechanics of making media are pretty simple. What's important is learning how to communicate with people effectively, because in the entertainment business you have to get other people to see your vision and get on board. Making movies and television isn't like writing a novel where you go off by yourself. It's all about team building, training people, and building consensus.

B&S: Can you find significance through all of this?

MW: In terms of significance, I think it's dangerous to look for significance and meaning through your work, whatever that is. Significance in life comes from walking uprightly and humbly before God. I know a lot of people in this business whose whole concept of significance is in their work; when their work goes away, they're just devastated, because they no longer have meaning. If your meaning is in the fact that you produce this or that hit show, well, all shows get canceled eventually, no matter how good they are.

B&S: After all these years in Hollywood your family is intact and you've got a great relationship with your kids. How did you do it?

MW: Working on a half-hour weekly comedy show is very time intensive. It's a sixty-hour work week, and you work late two nights in the writing process, and then you shoot a third night of the week. Years ago when my kids were small and I was a writer on *Happy Days,* I was leaving the house in the morning before my kids got up, and I came home after they had gone to bed. I asked myself, "Do I really want to exchange knowing my own children for success in the television business?" So I went to the studio and Garry Marshall, the producer, and said I needed to be home by 6:00. I fully anticipated that he would send me home right then. But Garry agreed, and he let me go home at six o'clock. Understand, you can't produce a TV show like that, but you can write. So for six years that's what I did, until my kids got older. Now, twenty years later, the dividends are astounding. The truth is, the show is long gone, but the family is still there.

B&S: What if the young person just breaking into the business feels like he or she has to put in the long hours in order to get ahead?

MW: Honestly, there is a sense in which they will lose out. When you make decisions in life about what your priorities are, you have to realize that there is a cost. But the benefits far outweigh the costs. The other thing I find among young people is that they don't understand that there is a process of moving through any career path. There's always an entry level. Every film student wants to be the next Steven Spielberg, but they don't realize that number one, he's a genius. And number two, even directors who work in the business have gone through a training process. That's true of any profession, and there's great value to it.

Young people are impatient, and part of the reason is that we haven't done a very good job of telling them what happens between the ages of twenty and thirty. We haven't explained the process. It's not simply graduating from college and becoming Steven Spielberg. It's much more complicated than that. And it's an amazing experience. I wouldn't trade my six years of writing for *Happy Days* for anything. What I learned as a writer prepared me to be a better producer.

B&S: What is the meaning of life for you personally?

MW: I find meaning in how well I do being obedient to God. I've never had a five-year or a ten-year plan. For me the meaning of life is to get up in the morning and say, "Lord, what should I do today?" and then to respond to that with integrity. And then when you go to bed at night, you known you've been able to touch and help and serve some people. I find much more fulfillment in my relationships than I do making TV shows.

THE SOUL OF THE CITY

Hollywood has the reputation of being a cutthroat town. At least that's what we had heard before we got there. So we expected to find a place where everyone climbs over the little people on their way to the top. (Bruce took particular offense at that notion because he insists that he's not little; he's just growth delayed.) But we found a Hollywood that defies its reputation.

We are sure that there is lots of phoniness, shallowness, and superficiality in Hollywood. It probably happens at those parties where everyone is trying to schmooze the next movie deal. But we didn't see any of that when we were there. Perhaps that's because we didn't get invited to any of those kinds of parties. (The closest we came was being in the crowd at the grand opening of a Krispy Kreme donut shop in Southern California. But the security guard wouldn't let us pass the rope to get into the store because he said we didn't have "the look" they were going for.)

The people we talked to in the Hollywood area were genuine and sincere. We were impressed that they felt a sense of responsibility for their part in producing the entertainment that influences our culture. We were also impressed that they were willing to give helpful advice to people considering a career in the entertainment field. (If there is a back-stabbing, cutthroat aspect to Hollywood, these people are not part of it.)

The Power of Cinema

How can a medium that is barely 100 years old evoke such interest and emotion in people around the world? Writer and director Scott Derrickson explained that film unites every great art form into one.

- Film has the aesthetic beauty of painting and photography
- Film has the emotional impact of theater and drama
- Film has the ability to take the audience up into the face of the actors
- Film has the quality of literature
- Film has the manipulative abilities of music

Put all of that into one art form and you have cinema, an incredibly powerful medium.

We compiled a list of the advice that was given to us by our new Hollywood friends. These words of guidance were directed toward young men and women in their twenties and thirties who might be considering a career in the entertainment business. Even if you're not in that particular age bracket, or if you're just content with your boring job as the Director of Global Operations for Nike, we think you'll find the list intriguing on several levels. First of all, it identifies the issues that people struggle with in Hollywood to produce quality entertainment. Second, it highlights the aspect of personal choice that confronts everyone—whether you are producing the entertainment or merely watching it. Third, and perhaps most important, this list reveals an interconnectedness between entertainment and the meaning of life.

Here is the list we refer to as the Hollywood Seven. We have included the explanation that was given with each instruction.

Society's hope is in your hands. The baby boomers had a vision of America that hasn't worked. They don't see their own failures, but the millennial generation does. If our society is going to reverse a downward spiral, it must come from this younger generation that is willing to put the good of the group ahead of their own personal gratification.

We have to change our minds before we can change our culture. Cultural decline is not effectively reversed by boycotts. It is accomplished by changing our attitudes. If we want to return to a values-based society, we must stop depicting mass murderers as cinematic heroes and finding humor in adulterous scenes in sitcoms. We should produce entertainment that tells the truth about human life, but it should inspire us to a higher level of integrity.

Don't neglect your craft and don't sell out. As a culture, we have succumbed to the weight of our mediocrity. We need to commit ourselves to excellence in our artistic endeavors. Innovation and imagination are critical. Master the fundamentals of your craft, then be creative and innovative within those disciplines. Furthermore, never compromise the content or quality of your work for style. Stay true to your spiritual convictions. There is no acceptable compromise on matters of integrity.

Hold on to the empowering inner voice. Keep listening to the voice of God within you. Do not compare yourself with others. Don't be market driven. Follow God's leading.

Think local and think relational. You are doomed for disappointment, dis-

couragement, and failure if you attempt to change the world with grand ideologies. God hasn't given the world to you, but he has given to you a close
circle of friends and associates. Be a redemptive influence within that small
group. Focus on personal relationships. They are what give validity to your
efforts.

Realize that things take time. Nothing happens overnight. Your efforts
won't be influential from the very start. You might not even get a job at the
very start. You don't graduate one day and start working with Steven
Spielberg the next. It takes a while. God works in mysterious ways. Be
patient, but work diligently in the meanwhile.

Understand the power of a story. Scott Derrickson told us that "story is
everything." There's no deeper way for us to convey truth and understand
ourselves other than through good stories. "The reason why Jesus ministered
with stories was because people interact with stories differently than they
interact with statements or ideas or platitudes," Scott said. "Stories allow people to get in there and swim around, and they become cocreators in the
process."

Each time we review that list we feel a closer connection with Hollywood.
And we also are continually amazed at how well those points apply to life in
the world that lies beyond the view of the HOLLYWOOD sign (which could
be less than a mile away on a smog-alert day).

departure
09731

NEXT STOP: LAS VEGAS

11

arrival mileage

I 0 0 2 7

LAS VEGAS:
Finding the Love of Your Life

Although it had been more than fourteen weeks since we began our search for the meaning of life in Boston, we couldn't end it in Hollywood. We had to push on—for several reasons.

First, we needed to sort out what we had learned. We had to clear our heads, and you can't do that in Hollywood. There are too many distractions.

Second, Stan was too susceptible to the Hollywood culture. He ditched the Dockers and cotton short-sleeve shirts he had been wearing for the entire trip in exchange for Levi's, a T-shirt, and a blazer. And he was speaking in the Hollywood vernacular, referring to doing lunch and taking a meeting. The severity of the problem became obvious to both of us when Stan told Bruce to "have your people contact my people." It sounded smooth, but each of us is the only "people" that the other guy's got.

Third, and most important, we didn't yet have a definitive answer to the meaning-of-life question. We knew we were close, but it hadn't come together. In each city we had focused on components of what might be the answer, but we needed to step back and get a broader perspective. It was time to let our thoughts coagulate, and that had to happen before we returned home to families, mortgages, and jobs.

We had arrived in Hollywood from the north, so our options for moving on were limited. We couldn't travel west. The Pacific Ocean is a formidable barrier when your sole mode of transportation is a car. We couldn't travel south. Oh, sure, the beaches of Ensenada, Mexico would be conducive for thought coagulation. And although we didn't have our passports with us, we were confident that getting across the border wouldn't be a problem for us since Stan had this suave Hollywood image thing working for him. But we didn't want to risk dealing with a vehicle breakdown south of the border. The rental contract didn't cover the car outside the United States, so we would be left to our own resources if there were a mechanical failure. Each of us has a difficult time understanding the mysteries of auto mechanics in English, and we knew that the cost of repair would increase exponentially, as the only sentence either of us speak fluently in Spanish is: "No hablo Espanol."

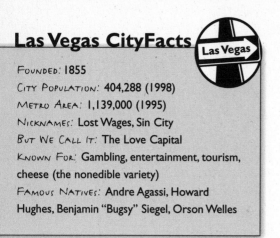

Las Vegas CityFacts

FOUNDED: 1855
CITY POPULATION: 404,288 (1998)
METRO AREA: 1,139,000 (1995)
NICKNAMES: Lost Wages, Sin City
BUT WE CALL IT: The Love Capital
KNOWN FOR: Gambling, entertainment, tourism, cheese (the nonedible variety)
FAMOUS NATIVES: Andre Agassi, Howard Hughes, Benjamin "Bugsy" Siegel, Orson Welles

We had no choice but to drive east.

When you're driving east out of Hollywood, the palm trees give way to cactus. Before long, you're smack dab in the middle of the Mojave Desert. We aren't desert people. Some folks love it, but we don't. (Based on the sparse population of desert communities like Barstow, Banning, and Blythe, most people are like us.) But there is one good thing about driving east across the Mojave Desert: Las Vegas is on the other side.

A TOWN THAT IS OVER THE TOP

The utter desolation that surrounds Las Vegas makes it all the more amazing. There's nothing geographically redeeming within two hundred miles of Las Vegas, yet it is a thriving metropolis. How can such dramatic growth occur in a region that appears to have no resource other than sand? The answer is obvious when you see the billboards as you approach the city. Las Vegas is more than a city. Las Vegas is even more than the leading gambling Mecca in the world. Las Vegas is outlandish, over the top, and overdone in every conceivable way. Nothing about it is understated.

Of course, it didn't start out that way. The Mormons founded Las Vegas in 1855 (how's that for irony?), but the town remained a sleepy settlement until 1931, when two significant events changed Las Vegas for good. First, the

Bureau of Reclamation started construction of Boulder Dam (later named Hoover Dam), then the largest in the world. The project brought a huge influx of jobs, development, and federal funds to Las Vegas. Second, the state of Nevada legalized gambling. Hotel and motel construction didn't begin in earnest until after World War II (gangster Bugsy Siegel's landmark Flamingo Casino started it all in 1945), and even then it took a while for Las Vegas to catch on as anything more than a watering hole.

By the early 1950s, Las Vegas was still little more than a novelty stop that offered a little gambling, a few burlesque shows, and some nightclub performers. There were only about eighteen hundred hotel rooms in Las Vegas back in 1953 (when you could get a regular room for $3, or splurge and get the deluxe room for a whopping $7.50 per night). For decades, Las Vegas had a reputation for being a raunchy, sleazy place, but in a cheesy kind of way. You went there looking for slots and suds, crooners and casinos, topless bars and bottomless buffets. This was certainly not a place for family entertainment. But that was then and this is now. Everything about Las Vegas has changed, thanks to three things.

THE HOTELS

This isn't your father's Las Vegas anymore (not that our fathers ever went there). Now there are more than 120,000 hotel rooms (with an 86 percent annual occupancy rate). Gone are most of the dive motels that populated the north end of Las Vegas Boulevard. The action is now at the south end (also known as The Strip), where some of the glitziest, largest, and most expensive hotels in the world have been built in the last ten years. Gambling is still big business in Las Vegas, but there's much more to this desert oasis than roulette wheels and poker tables.

Unlike every other major city, where hotels are built to accommo-

America's Most Popular Vacation Cities

When Americans go on vacation, these are their favorite cities (in descending order):

ORLANDO

NEW YORK CITY

LAS VEGAS

NEW ORLEANS

date the visitors who come to see the tourist attractions, the hotels *are* the attractions in Las Vegas. Actually, to describe them as "hotels" is an unjust understatement (unless we're talking about the few remaining "old school" hotels such as Harrah's, the Tropicana, or the Flamingo Hilton, which we aren't). The new attractions of Las Vegas are the themed resorts. The resort renaissance was already well underway in 1998 when casino mogul Steve Wynn opened the elegant $1.6 billion Bellagio, the most expensive hotel ever constructed at the time. In addition to a full-blown convention center, a gambling area the size of a football field, and a world-class spa, the Bellagio featured its own fine art gallery with a collection of paintings valued at more than $400 million. In the two years that followed the introduction of the Bellagio, Las Vegas citizens and tourists witnessed the opening of:

- The aquatic-themed Mandalay Bay, with its own beach and eleven-acre lagoon;
- The Venetian Resort Hotel and Casino, complete with singing gondoliers navigating their authentic gondolas in the canals that meander through the hotel;
- The Paris Las Vegas hotel, with a half-scale Eiffel Tower; and
- The glitzy Aladdin Resort and Casino, with its Middle Eastern theme.

Lacking the panache of the new themed resorts, the older hotels are being remodeled or replaced. (Actually, they are being blown up. The biggest show in Las Vegas occurs every so often when they implode an old hotel in order to make room for a new one.) In 1998 the antiquated Aladdin was imploded and rebuilt and had its grand reopening shortly before we arrived. The fifty-year-old Desert Inn was also closed because Steve Wynn has plans to build a skyscraper hotel on the site that will be the tallest on The Strip and more opulent than the Bellagio, which he no longer owns.

A drive down Las Vegas Boulevard South might leave you thinking that creative possibilities for themed resorts have been exhausted, because in addition to those we've already mentioned, there are:

- The Luxor Hotel and Casino—all things Egyptian, including hotel rooms packed into a pyramid large enough to cover a 747;
- The Excalibur Hotel and Casino—nights with knights;
- The MGM Grand Hotel and Casino—more movie memorabilia than in Hollywood and, with more than five thousand rooms, the second biggest hotel in the world;

• New York New York Hotel and Casino—the Big Apple with a roller coaster circling a one-third-size Statue of Liberty;

• Caesars Palace—a first-century Roman theme, only here the barmaids wear togas that were influenced by the miniskirt craze of the 1970s;

• Mirage Las Vegas Resort—a South Seas hotel, complete with exotic fish and white tigers;

• Treasure Island at The Mirage—like spending the night in Disneyland's Pirates of the Caribbean.

But if you think there are no more possibilities, you're wrong. At the time of our visit, we read of plans for:

• A "City by the Bay" resort—a San Francisco theme with a Vegas version of the Golden Gate Bridge; and

• A resort with a *Titanic* theme—putting the casino in the iceberg and time-share condos in the fake smokestacks.

The Las Vegas themed resorts aren't just about hotel rooms and casinos. One of the newest attractions of Las Vegas is "shoppertainment." It all started with the Forum Shops at Caesar's Palace—the most financially successful retail center in the United States. Bellagio features very high-end boutique stores, the Venetian has its Grand Canal Shoppes, and the Aladdin has an enclosed, mile-long theme retail-dining complex called the Desert Passage. You still see a few discount souvenir and T-shirt shops, but the only people shopping here are those who have lost their own shirts gambling.

THE SHOWS

Las Vegas is known for its hotels and is also famous for its shows. Ever since the Rat Pack invaded The Strip with its kooky, crazy brand of drunken revelry, entertainers from all levels of show business have come to Las Vegas to perform in hotel lounges and theaters. Actually, the entertainers come from only two levels of show business: unknown and over-the-hill. You won't find the top musical acts in Vegas. The people here are either on their way up or on their way down. If a singer or a group has a number-one hit, they don't play the Mirage or the MGM Grand. Las Vegas hotels are filled with the likes of Frankie Avalon, Isaac Hayes, the Smothers Brothers, and Duran Duran.

America's Fastest-Growing City

While thirty million people visit Las Vegas each year, more than seventy-five thousand move to this desert metropolis annually, making it the fastest-growing city in America. They come for the jobs, the affordable housing, the low tax rate (there's no corporate or personal income tax, thanks to those tourist dollars), and the sun. The population of greater Las Vegas reached a million in 1994, and if present trends continue there will be two million residents by 2005. The phone company has to issue two local directories each year.

Of course, if you just have to see a superstar perform, you can, as long as you don't mind seeing a poor imitation of the real thing. We're talking about celebrity impersonators, who apparently make a decent living in Las Vegas (our impression is that Las Vegas is the imitation celebrity capital of the world). We saw an ad for one show featuring Michael Jackson, Madonna, Ricky Martin, Reba McEntire, and Elvis—all for only thirty-eight dollars, including dinner! Even in the world of fake celebrities, Elvis is king. We noticed at least three shows dedicated to Elvis: Viva Elvis, Aloha Elvis, and our personal favorite, the Elvis-A-Rama Show and Museum.

As for the up-and-coming entertainers, there are plenty of those to go around, and in many cases they are some of the hottest acts in town. If you've never been to Las Vegas, you've probably never heard of Danny Gans. But if you ever go and you ask the locals to recommend the best show in town, the majority will tell you to see Danny Gans at the Mirage. Now, we didn't see Danny Gans (mainly because his two nightly shows were sold out all week), but we have it on good report that this guy (who is an impersonator—what else?) is clean, funny, and very talented. He's also been voted the top entertainer in Las Vegas for the last two years.

Since we only had a couple of nights in Las Vegas, we opted for something we knew: the Blue Man Group. That's right, the boys in blue have their own show and theater in the Luxor, and even though the Las Vegas version lacks the intimacy and funky off-Broadway feel of the New York version, it's great fun (and hugely popular). The only other Las Vegas shows we would recommend are the two Cirque du Soleil extravaganzas: *O* at Bellagio and *Mystere* at Treasure Island. Take your pick. Both shows are amazing, expensive (more than $100 a pop—we're not joking), and truly memorable (mainly because they are so amazing and expensive).

THE FOOD

Until a few years ago, food in Las Vegas could be summarized in one word: buffet. And not just any ordinary, hometown buffet. We're talking enough food to feed Patton's army, spread out in mile-long self-serve counters (protected by Plexiglas sneeze shields, thank goodness) in order to serve thousands of people per hour—all for just $5.95. Sure, you could get a prime rib dinner for only $3.95, but why limit yourself to meat and vegetables, when you can eat yourself sick from every food group in the known universe?

There are still plenty of buffets in Las Vegas—every hotel has one, and there's always a line—but the big food attraction these days is the gourmet restaurant. In an effort to attract the elusive and always desirable "high roller," the mega hotels got the bright idea a few years back to recruit the finest restaurateurs in the world to open up signature eateries. Wolfgang Puck was the first really big name to establish a food foothold in Las Vegas, and now there are at least a half dozen world-class restaurants in Las Vegas.

Of course, these places are no buffet bargain. The prices on the menus of Mobil five-star restaurants like Bellagio's Picasso and Renoir in the Mirage will lighten your wallet as much as the top-notch shows (which is why we opted to eat at the buffets). So beware. Even if you never put a dollar in the slots, Las Vegas will get your money one way or another.

LOOKING FOR MEANING IN THE MIDST OF THE GLITZ

Since we were at the end of our trip, we didn't have any money left, so most of what Las Vegas has to offer wasn't much of a temptation for us. Besides, we had a job to finish. Just as we had done in each of the other ten cities we visited, we were compelled to search for the meaning of life. This should not have been a problem. In virtually every other city a theme of some kind emerged within the first few hours of our arrival. Not so with Las Vegas. After twenty-four hours, we still didn't have a handle on what Las Vegas was all about and what it had to do with the meaning of life.

We wondered if we were missing the heart and soul of Las Vegas by confining our search to The Strip. Should we be focusing on one of the Las Vegas suburbs, where everyday citizens live their lives? We quickly rejected that idea. Suburbs are suburbs, whether you're in Las Vegas or Chicago. No, if we couldn't find the meaning of life on The Strip—the one place that defines Las Vegas—we weren't going to find it. The way we figured it, we just weren't looking hard enough, or there was something so obvious that we couldn't see it.

That's when we decided to jump in a cab with our video camera and note pad. "Drive us to the end of The Strip," we told the driver, a rather outgoing guy in his early thirties. "And tell us everything you know about this town. We're looking for the meaning of life."

We've said this before, but we'll say it again. No topic of conversation opens up communication lines with other people—regardless of age, profession, ethnicity, or spiritual orientation—better than the meaning of life. It's amazing how easy it is for people to talk about it. Our cab driver for the next hour was very talkative, and without even knowing it he led us straight to the meaning we were looking for.

As he drove north on Las Vegas Boulevard, we asked questions and took notes, looking for something to define the meaning of this city. The usual things popped into our vision first (at least they're usual for Las Vegas), mainly because they're designed to grab your attention.

The hotels. We passed them all, even the boarded-up Desert Inn and the odd-looking Stratosphere Tower (that's the very tall and very thin hotel with the roller coaster at the top). The hotels are impressive as you drive by, even if you're in a Dodge Caravan cab rather than a stretch limo, but they don't give you a clue as to the meaning of life.

The lights. Even if you cruise The Strip during the day, you notice the lights and the gigantic signs beckoning you into each hotel and casino like enormous neon barkers. We were cruising at night, when the lights are beyond dazzling. To us they looked like living electronic organisms with minds of their own. We marveled at the sheer wattage required to drive the lights of Las Vegas (we even wondered how many people are employed full-time just to change the bulbs). We marveled and we wondered, but we didn't find the meaning of life among the lights.

The water. For a desert city that receives less than five inches of rainfall a year, you sure see a lot of water around. All the hotels have elaborate pools and fountains, and some—like the Bellagio and the Mirage—have spectacu-lar water shows that leave you breathless. We didn't see any meaning there, but the use of water is interesting, especially when you learn that the hotels are required to use recycled water for their big aquatic spectacles.

So much for the superficial part of Las Vegas. We kept looking for mean-ing as we went below the surface.

The people. There are a lot of cars driving the six lanes of the 4.5 mile length of The Strip at any given moment, but you don't really notice the cars as much as the people. Just like Fifth Avenue in New York, Michigan Avenue in Chicago, and Main Street in Disney World, there are thousands upon thou-sands of people walking along Las Vegas Boulevard. We could only assume that they were walking from hotel to hotel, because you certainly can't do any window shopping on The Strip. No, these people were just like us, wandering around taking in the sights. We didn't see much meaning in that.

The money. Las Vegas must be the only place left in the world where you can lay your eyes on real cash. Everywhere else you see plastic (as in credit cards). Not here. In Las Vegas, cash is king (which is why we are mere peas-ants in this kingdom). We didn't see any cash on our cab tour of The Strip, but the evidence of money is everywhere. The hotel rooms, the restaurants, the shows, and especially the gambling feed Las Vegas with a seemingly end-less money stream. But people here aren't looking for meaning in their money, at least not in the same way a Wall Street investment banker or a Microsoft millionaire might look for it. Money in Las Vegas is merely the means for something else people are seeking.

WE FOUND IT!

Our cab driver had taken us near the north end of The Strip, and we were running out of options. Here there aren't any themed resort hotels (think motels by the hour instead), and the lights are pretty dim. The only water you see is the runoff from the window air conditioners. Yet in the middle of this less-glam-orous part of Las Vegas is something that made us sit up and take notice. Scattered between the adult bookstores and rundown apartment buildings were several—make that dozens—of wedding chapels. You heard us. Wedding chapels, with names like the Little White Wedding Chapel, the Viva Las Vegas Wedding Chapel, and the Drive-Through Tunnel of Love Wedding Chapel.

In fact, there are more than fifty wedding chapels in Las Vegas, and that doesn't count the chapels located in each resort hotel on The Strip. More than 100,000 couples come to Las Vegas to get married each year, mainly because

WEDDING KNIGHTS

Like everything else about Las Vegas, the wedding industry is over the top. Any city can offer the traditional, plain-old weddings with tuxedos for the groomsmen and chiffon dress for the bridesmaids. But in Las Vegas, the "traditional" wedding has Elvis singing a few songs (and perhaps officiating at the ceremony).

Although themed wedding chapels are about as plentiful in Las Vegas as slot machines and showgirls, nothing tops the quick-change artistry of the Viva Las Vegas Wedding Chapel. This place can give you whatever ambiance and setting you can imagine, but it has about fifteen standard themes to choose from if your creativity is clogged. We'll skip over the more mundane themes (such as Victorian, gangster, and Western) and tell you about our favorites:

Intergalactic Wedding: Your ceremony takes place in the Starship Chapel, and the name of the minister is either Captain James T. Quirk or Mr. Schpock (the choice is yours). The wedding guests include life-size cutouts of your favorite space characters. The seven-hundred-dollar package includes a transporter and one illusion entrance "as you prepare to enter your new life, going places no man has gone before."

Harley Wedding: Your $725 fee includes a two-hour rental of two Harley-Davidson motorcycles, so you can drive up to the altar and then cruise the strip after the ceremony. (Oil drip pans in the chapel are extra.)

Camelot Wedding: Imagine Merlin as your minister with strolling minstrels singing medieval tunes as you walk down the aisle of the castle. For an extra charge, knights and fair ladies can be added to your guests.

Elvis's Blue Hawaii: Performed in the Elvis Chapel, this ceremony guarantees one genuine Elvis impersonator as the minister, and your choice of two hula dancers, two showgirls, or a Priscilla impersonator. Theatrical lighting and fog are also included as part of the ceremony. You get a souvenir cassette recording of songs sung by Elvis. Thank you, thank you very much.

the city makes it as easy as buying a lottery ticket. A marriage license costs thirty-five dollars, no blood test is required, and there's no waiting period. The Bureau of Licensing stays open until midnight on weekdays and twenty-four hours on weekends. The wedding chapels never close.

So couples of all kinds and from all around the world come here to get married. Actually, it makes you feel kind of warm and fuzzy inside. In a culture where love and commitment are discarded like yesterday's news, it's rather heartwarming to realize that in Las Vegas hundreds of couples every day—twenty-five hundred on Valentine's Day alone—believe that marriage still counts for something (even if an Elvis impersonator pronounces you man and wife).

As we drove past the Drive-Through Tunnel of Love Wedding Chapel, we asked our cab driver to stop. We had spotted a couple standing beneath the Tunnel of Love, and we decided to ask them some questions. Now you have to understand that the Drive-Through Tunnel of Love Wedding Chapel is just what the name says. This is the one place in Las Vegas (and in the world, we suspect) where you can drive up in your car and get married at the drive-through window. It's as easy as ordering two burgers and two Diet Cokes.

The unsuspecting couple was standing by the window, because their big rigs wouldn't fit under the Tunnel of Love (maximum height: 10' 6"). You see, they were truck drivers who had met just five weeks earlier, and they had come to Las Vegas to get married—her for the third time and him for the fourth. They thought it would be appropriate to get married in their trucks. Only they had to settle for standing in front of the drive-through marriage window instead of actually driving through. It was sweet. They were sweet.

"So why get married?" we asked them.

"We want to demonstrate our love," she replied. "And this time it's going to stick." She looked at soon-to-be husband number three. He looked back at her lovingly and smiled. That's when it hit us like a roll of silver dollars. Standing there in the Drive-Through Tunnel of Love Wedding Chapel at ten o'clock in the evening with our Caravan cab driver parked by the curb and this couple from the American road standing there, wanting very much for this marriage to be the one that works—that's when we figured it out. The meaning of life in Las Vegas isn't about the money or the glitz. It isn't even about wedding chapels and marriage. In Las Vegas the meaning of life is love.

THE FLYING ELVI ARE ALIVE AND WELL

Elvis Presley has been dead for almost twenty-five years, but you would never know that in Las Vegas. More than a few guys make their living impersonating Elvis, there's the Elvis-A-Rama Museum, and now there's even a group of ten Elvis impersonators who call themselves The Flying Elvi. That's right, grown men dressed up in the classic Elvis Las Vegas costume (you know the one; a white jumpsuit with rhinestones, a big belt buckle, and oversized collar) are in demand across the country, mainly at ballparks and grand openings. The group was formed after the movie *Honeymoon in Vegas* introduced the idea. Long live the king!

Hundreds of thousands of people come to this city-in-the-middle-of-nowhere each year to get married. Millions more come as couples celebrating anniversaries and other special occasions, or just to have a weekend together. Others come as singles looking for something meaningful that they don't have at home. When you get right down to it, they're all here looking for the same thing: the love and affection and approval of someone who accepts them just the way they are.

We had new inspiration as we wished our trucker friends God's blessings and got back in our cab. "Take us back to our hotel," we said. "We've found what we're looking for." We couldn't wait to interview more people about love and marriage. We woke up bright and early the next day and checked the schedule of weddings in the chapel at our hotel, and we saw several on the list, starting at ten o'clock in the morning. Flush with excitement, we positioned ourselves in the corridor outside the wedding chapel, video camera and notebooks in hand, eager to talk to more couples in love.

DÉJÀ VU ALL OVER AGAIN

It wasn't easy to get a bride or groom to talk to us. Throughout the morning we saw brides and bridal attendants in all their wedding regalia walking down the corridors, either to or from the wedding chapel. We spotted grooms and groomsmen, all decked out in great-looking tuxes. In each case, however, the wedding couples were either leaving the ceremony on their way to the reception, or they were leaving the reception on their way to the Honeymoon Suite. Either way, we didn't have a chance. The brides were tense and focused on the next event, and the grooms were in some kind of daze. Besides, none of them was willing to spare even a few minutes to talk to two guys flush with excitement, holding a video camera and note pads.

Since we couldn't talk to the brides and grooms, we did the next best thing. We talked to the hotel's wedding concierge, which turned out to be a pretty good idea. After all, these concierges are professional know-it-alls. Or at least they want you to think so. Many of them are arrogant and aloof (think Martin Short's Franck character from *Father of the Bride*), but we found a really nice one. He didn't even use a fake French accent. This concierge told us that there are basically two types of people who choose to get married in the nicer wedding accommodations.

There are the "first-timers." These are usually young couples who are getting married for the first time, and the bride's father is rich enough to fly the entire wedding party and all the guests to Las Vegas for the extravaganza. (Obviously these people are getting married in one of the elegant hotel wedding chapels rather than the Elvis Hunk O' Burning Love Chapel.) Often, these weddings are as much a tribute to the father's net worth as they are a celebration of conjugal commitment.

And there are the "second-timers." These are usually older couples, each of whom have been married and divorced, but who are now entering the matrimonial waters for a second time. Their wedding ceremonies are attended by fewer guests; usually just a few close friends. They still want a degree of elegance, but they dispense with a lot of the hoopla. (We understood that to mean that the reception is celebrated around the roulette table.)

We found it very interesting that a small but significant portion of the "second-timers" form a subset called "déjà vu'ers" (divorced couples who are getting married again to each other—sometimes on their original anniversary date). We asked our wise concierge for his insights about this déjà vu'er phenomenon. In his omniscient opinion, these couples got divorced in the first place because they allowed the demands of parenthood, careers, and the household to take priority over their marriage. Over time, the quality of their relationship deteriorated. But, the reality of separation and divorce often instigates reflection on the importance of the relationship itself.

This concierge was of the opinion that these déjà vu'er marriages will be stronger than many first-timer marriages and will be more resistant to divorce (a second time) because the couple has a deeper understanding of what it will take for their relationship to endure through the circumstances of life. We asked him to speculate on how the déjà vu'ers might answer our meaning-of-life question. Without hesitating, he replied: "For them, the meaning of life must involve their newfound understanding of commitment to each other."

We thought these were very discerning insights that obviously hadn't been part of the concierge's training at hotel-management school. We asked how he came to such keen perceptions. As it turns out, he was a déjà vu'er himself. Ahh, there is nothing like wisdom gained the hard way.

IS LOVE A MYTH?

After spending three days—and a lot of money—in Las Vegas, it's important to do a reality check. You can easily lose all sense of time and perspective in a city designed to take you away from the real world (nothing closes and there are no clocks visible in any public places). For some people, a reality check involves the realization that excessive gambling, drinking, and carousing are frowned upon in Des Moines. For others it means you can't eat yourself into a carbohydrate stupor once you return home. Our reality check was a little different. As we prepared to leave Las Vegas and conclude our meaning-of-life odyssey, we wanted to make sure that love really was the theme we were looking for. More critically, we wanted to know if love is still a big deal in the lives of everyday people—not just in Las Vegas, but everywhere. We must admit we had our doubts.

As cultural observers, our job is to talk to people, but we also make it a point to scour the media looking for clues to the way people find meaning. While we were in Washington, we read an article by a single female lamenting the lack of datable men in our nation's capital. According to this journalist, dating in D.C. is futile because most of the single men are either gay or disgruntled unemployed lawyers. Even though we couldn't identify with her rather cynical and somewhat tongue-in-cheek viewpoint (each of us is happily married and at least one of us is a gruntled employed lawyer), we could clearly read between the lines. Dating, love, and marriage aren't easy to come by in a large city.

While we were in Los Angeles, we heard about a new concept called SpeedDating. Concerned over the lack of social interaction between men and women, a Jewish educational group started a service where single Jewish men and women can pay $25 for an evening of social interaction. Couples pair off and get seven minutes to "date" each other. At the end of the allotted time, a bell rings, and everyone has to move on to another partner, but not before checking "yes" or "no" on a card. If both check "yes," then phone numbers are exchanged and a real date is arranged. The concept has become so popular that SpeedDating has been trademarked and licensed in twenty-five cities around the world. Is it possible to find love in such an environment? Only time (and we're talking more than seven minutes here) will tell.

In opposition to the creative methods some men and women are engaging

Looking for Love in Digital Places

In a city with thirty million visitors and seventy-five thousand new residents coming in each year, it's difficult to establish meaningful relationships. At least that's what we were told. Rather than cruising The Strip for dates, the locals have become much more sophisticated in their search for love. In a word, they've gone digital. We were told that free and fee-based Internet dating services are quite the rage. (These are not unique to Las Vegas. They are available in your hometown, but your search can be limited to your locale.)

The people we talked to seemed pretty intent about using these on-line dating services. They said it is easy and efficient, although the odds are against finding the love of your life. (Leave it to people in Las Vegas to put odds on everything.) When our conversation wound around to our chosen topic, they told us that love was a big part of the meaning of life. It was interesting to us that they spoke about the meaning of life in the future tense. Like love, they didn't have it yet, but they were sure that it would come. It just took finding the right person to make the whole thing work.

Maybe we are traditionalists. We think that finding the love of your life ought to be done the old-fashioned way: either you see someone you're interested in and pursue a relationship, or you get Chuck Woolery involved.

these days to simply meet each other, there is another trend that seems to be growing among young adults. It's the trend of the single life. Of course, we were aware of the effects of divorce on our culture, but we figured that most divorced people want to eventually get married again (and again). Not so. If we're reading this correctly, the new trend seems to be for divorced or never-married adults to stay single. And the trend seems to be stronger with women than men.

So where does love fit into all of this? Well, it's not at the top of everyone's list. When asked what they missed most about not being married, more than three-quarters of both men and women didn't list love or sex, but "companionship." Teresa Moore, a writer who lives in San Francisco, wrote this in *UnderWire,* an Internet magazine: "Perhaps what I really love best about my life is the adventure of making it up as I go along. I am the author of my days. I have a good net—friends and loved ones in many quarters—so I don't mind traveling without a map."

Is love a myth in our culture today? Certainly it is if you focus on media portrayals and big-city trends. But is that where real people live? Yes, increasing numbers of people are living in cities, and urban centers like New York and Hollywood and Las Vegas seem to drive much of our popular culture. But do big-city life and big-city values represent what the rest of us are looking for? A popular country song once said, "I'm looking for love in all the wrong places." Perhaps the reason love is a myth in our culture is that people don't know where to look. We almost made that mistake, looking for love in the lights and glamour of Las Vegas. We didn't find it until we went below the surface and looked into the faces of the truck-driving couple at the Drive-Through Tunnel of Love Wedding Chapel.

SOUL OF THE CITY

Maybe we were exhausted from the entire cross-country trip. Maybe we weren't thinking clearly because at this point we had had "meaning of life" on the brain for fourteen straight weeks. Maybe we were being lulled into a semicomatose state by the pools and fountains of Las Vegas (not to mention feeling bloated from the all-you-can-eat buffets). Whatever it was, both of us agreed that Las Vegas was an appropriate end to our search. It didn't give us an entire, solitary answer for the meaning of life, but its theme of love certainly got us to thinking about something that could very well be a foundation for the answer. We decided to think a little deeper.

We aren't novices on the subject of love (although our wives may dispute this contention). We've both had some limited prior exposure to the ancient Greek and Latin languages (which had been refreshed by our visits to Caesar's Palace), so we remembered that the Greek and Roman cultures categorized love with three separate definitions—all of which we noticed in Las Vegas:

Eros: This is the physical aspect of love—the lust part. Erotic comes from the same root word. There is no shortage of examples of eros love in Las Vegas. The strip clubs, topless bars, and adult book stores at the north end of the strip are evidence enough. But we sure didn't get the impression that there was any meaning of life in any of that. Although our contact with such places was limited to driving by on our taxi tour, the entire scene was pretty depressing.

Philos: This involves the type of love that is shared between friends. The name Philadelphia comes from this root word. (Get it? Philadelphia . . . the city of brotherly love.) There is closeness and a spirit of camaraderie that underlies philos love. This is an enjoyable type of connection, but it isn't necessarily long lasting. It is often a bond that can be broken by circumstances.

Agape: This is the ultimate level of love. It is a self-sacrificing love, a love that puts a higher priority on the welfare of the other person than on your own desires. Agape love is the type of love that is used to describe God's love for mankind. While we aren't prepared to say that any person can have a love that matches God's, maybe the couples in the déjà vu'er marriages are getting close. They are if they realize that their commitment (love) for each other should not be affected by external circumstances such as finances, careers, or kids. From what the concierge told us, those marriages often failed in the first place because each spouse demanded his or her own way. He was optimistic for the success of these marriages on the second round because the spouses had learned that love means being self-sacrificing instead of selfish. That is the essence of agape love.

The more we thought about it, the more we realized that love had been a recurring component in many of the responses we had obtained across our ten-thousand-mile trek. Very few people had given an outright answer of "love" when we asked them about the meaning of life. But when we reviewed and reflected on the replies we had been given across the country, love (of the philos or agape variety) seemed to be an implied element in many of the responses:

"Family"
"Friends"
"Relationships"
"Doing things for others."

We were talking about all of these things as we drove out of Las Vegas and headed toward home. As had become our custom driving through thirty states, we looked for clever bumper stickers and license plate frames wherever we were. (Through certain stretches of Texas that is the only way to stay awake on the freeway because the scenery certainly doesn't change.) Not too far outside of Las Vegas, we noticed a bumper sticker that read:

LOVE DOESN'T MAKE THE WORLD GO 'ROUND.
LOVE IS WHAT MAKES THE RIDE WORTHWHILE.

It was as if we had asked the driver about the meaning of life and she was giving us her reply. It was a pretty good answer, and we asked no more.

departure
10304

EPILOGUE

Any attempt to fully convey what we learned from our search about the meaning of life would be futile. How's that for the opening line of an epilogue? But don't give up on us or throw this book into the recycle bin out of disgust (or put it back on the shelf if you're standing in the bookstore trying to find the answer without buying this book). Hear us out.

In the Prologue of the book (that's the little section right before chapter 1 for those of you keeping score), we said that people are passionate about the meaning of life. The thing about passion is that it's very personal. Passion means different things to different people. For the truck-driving couple getting married in the Drive-Through Tunnel of Love Wedding Chapel, their passion was to make love work—once and for all. For Mako Fujimura, the New York artist, passion was a lifelong journey of expression. For Michael in New Orleans, it was a clean cab.

THE THREADS OF A TAPESTRY

We can't fully convey what we learned because the real impact comes from the synthesis of all our experiences together. It is the compilation of more than a thousand interviews and responses, which have permanently affected our perspective on life. Even as we write this book, months after our search ended, we can still see the faces and hear the voices of the people we talked to, and their answers are just as clear. (No, we don't possess psychic powers. We have fifteen cassettes of digital video.)

Each interview was like the thread of a tapestry. It had meaning and significance by itself, but no single response captured the full complexity of the answer. But when interwoven with all of the other "threads" we collected across the country, the result is a beautiful tapestry with a perspective about life that has richness, depth, and substance.

Let us give you an idea of the threads we collected along the way. Here are two of the thousands of images that are etched in our memory. As you read these brief accounts, you will see how each provides some insight into the meaning of life.

SPEECHLESS IN PORTLAND

In Portland we connected with the owner of a successful high-tech business. There was intensity and pressure in the air throughout the office as deals were being made and business was transacted. But behind the closed door of his private office, this business owner was still and somber. We had just asked him this question: "What is the meaning of life?"

He refused to answer. It wasn't a defiant refusal; just a defeated one. He said he couldn't respond because he didn't know the answer. Then he told us what had happened to him a week earlier:

> I WAS HAVING MY ANNUAL PHYSICAL. JUST WHEN I THOUGHT MY DOCTOR HAD FINISHED, HE SAID HE HAD ONE MORE QUESTION FOR ME. HE ASKED ME, "ARE YOU DOING WHAT YOU WERE PUT ON EARTH TO DO?" I COULDN'T GIVE HIM AN ANSWER. I JUST CRIED.

LETTING GO

We were continually amazed at people's hospitality. At one stop, we were invited to join a family as they celebrated the dad's fiftieth birthday at an Italian restaurant. Around the table sat three generations of this family: the grandfather, the mom and dad, and their children (ranging in ages from middle school to college). As the rest of us stuffed our faces with pizza, the dad rose from his seat to give a little speech. We could tell that he had been planning to use this occasion as an opportunity to teach a lesson to his children. Neither he nor we could have ever imagined that his comments would be so appropriate to our search:

I want to take this opportunity to tell you what I have learned about life. It's all about letting go. When you are a little kid, you learn to let go of your toys to share them with others. As a teenager, you let go of some of the things you want to do because your friends want to do something else. When you get married, you let go of financial support from your parents because you are starting your own family. Then, as you have kids of your own, life is a constant process of letting go of them in degrees as they get older and become more self-sufficient. As you become elderly, you are forced to let go of things like your health and your independence.

As I have been thinking about this, it seems to me that the process of letting go can be really depressing—unless you know whom you are letting go to. If you live your life in a vacuum without any spiritual connections, then you are losing whatever you are letting go. You can't get it back, and you feel like you have forfeited something that you used to hold dear. But if you are letting go of these things to God—realizing that he is in control of your life—then letting go means that things are getting better because they are within his plan.

So, whatever stage you're at in life, you need to learn to let go.

We looked at the kids around the table. Each of them gave their dad a respectful nod of their heads as they continued to shovel pizza into their mouths. We, on the other hand, sat motionless—as the pizza topping dripped from our chins—because we knew we had another thread for our tapestry.

WE WEREN'T THE FIRST TO SEARCH FOR THE MEANING OF LIFE

We had one panic attack on our journey. It happened in South Carolina. We were being interviewed on an AM radio talk show and answering questions from the local callers. Our gastric juices erupted when one caller said: "I don't know why you guys are on this search. Someone else has already done it. And he even wrote a book about it."

At moments of great shock, most people have visions of their lives flashing before their eyes. We each had a vision of our wives standing before us. "Why did you morons take this idiotic trip if you could have simply read some other guy's book?" we could hear them saying in unison. (We are married to different women, but they think alike.)

It turns out that the caller was yanking our chain—sort of. He told us that the guy he was referring to was King Solomon (the son of David, of David and Goliath fame). And the book that Solomon wrote was Ecclesiastes in the Bible. Even if Solomon asked the meaning-of-life question, his answers were now about three thousand years old. We suddenly felt better and didn't think that our search was redundant.

That caller prompted us to read Ecclesiastes. He was right. The entire book (only 237 verses) is about Solomon's search for meaning in life. If you thought our opening sentence of this Epilogue was lame, you won't like the opening line in Ecclesiastes any better:

EVERYTHING IS MEANINGLESS . . . UTTERLY MEANINGLESS.

We never got that negative and pessimistic. (Well, maybe in the oppressive heat of New Orleans in July, but our attitudes improved when we straddled the air conditioner in our hotel room.) Ecclesiastes is not as depressing a read as you might imagine. Solomon wrote it in his old age when he was regretting that much of his life had been wasted chasing after things that didn't really matter.

Our findings matched what Solomon was talking about. Although he was speaking from firsthand experience and we were getting our information second hand, many of our conclusions were the same. Based on our interviews, we agree with Solomon that the meaning of life is not found in:

Wealth. At the time of his reign, no one on earth was richer than Solomon. He bragged about his wealth but admitted that money and possessions by themselves aren't the answer. ("This is the case of a man who is all alone, without a child or a brother, yet who works hard to gain as much wealth as he can . . . . It is all so meaningless and depressing," Ecclesiastes 4:8.) We found no disagreement from the people we interviewed. We met with some very wealthy individuals (very wealthy). And the significance of the meaning of wealth popped into the conversations in many of the cities we visited, but no one suggested that meaning was found in money. If it had significance at all, it was only in how money could be used to help others.

Pleasure. Solomon could speak from experience about pleasure. Historians say that he had hundreds of wives and concubines. He admitted that he didn't deprive himself of any indulgence. ("I had everything a man could desire! . . . Anything I wanted, I took. I did not restrain myself from any joy. . . . There was nothing really worthwhile anywhere," Ecclesiastes 2:8, 10, 11.) We got the same impression in our search. Pleasure may give momentary satisfaction, but a life designed around pleasure will be empty. Only one person, of the more than one thousand we interviewed, gave a contrary response. It was in Seattle where a twenty-something guy told us that partying was the meaning of life. He was a driver for Budweiser beer, so we suspect that he might have been influenced by his company's own advertising (or under the influence of its product).

Work. We met many people who were extremely accomplished and successful in their careers. We are sure that many of them were workaholics. But no one ever said that they found meaning in the effort of work. Our findings coincided with Solomon's. ("I turned in despair from hard work. It was not the answer to my search for satisfaction in this life," Ecclesiastes 2:20.) Rather than work itself, the significance came from the benefit that the effort brought to the lives of other people.

Power. Solomon was perhaps the most powerful king of his day. Historians report that kings and leaders from other countries traveled to Jerusalem to learn from Solomon. Yet Solomon knew the futility of political power. ("He might become the leader of millions and be very popular. But then the next generation grows up and rejects him! So again, it is all meaningless, like chasing the wind," Ecclesiastes 4:16.) We met some very powerful people, particularly in Washington, D.C. and Hollywood. None of them ascribed any significance to their power as it related to the meaning of life. While their power afforded them practical advantages, it was meaningful to them only as it allowed them to be helpful in the lives of other people.

Wisdom. Solomon is described in the Bible as the wisest man who ever lived. He didn't find wisdom to give meaning to life. ("So of what value is all my wisdom? . . . This is all so meaningless," Ecclesiastes 2:15.) We met with a fair share of the wise and intellectual of our society, from university presidents to a Nobel laureate. None of these geniuses found life's meaning in their intellect. Dr. Charles Townes (whose Nobel prize is the closest we'll ever come to having one of our own) exudes intelligence, but he expressed the meaning of life in terms of training students and building relationships with them, and he said that love plays a part in the meaning of life.

Ecclesiastes is worth reading because Solomon included his conclusions about what he found to be meaningful in life. After a biographical tour of his futile attempts, he declares that he found meaning in knowing and obeying God. His comments about the emptiness of life are designed to prompt the reader to pursue God. We don't think he was trying to destroy hope, but to direct people to where they could find real hope.

We assure you that we haven't manipulated our findings to fit a certain agenda. We're laying them out for you as we heard them. But we do find it fascinating, and perhaps not coincidental, that the experiences that Solomon found to be meaningless are still proving to be void of ultimate meaning and satisfaction in our culture almost three thousand years later. Solomon—and the people we interviewed—placed significance on knowledge, wealth, work, power, and happiness, only when integrated in proper perspective. These temporal things only matter when life is seen in light of a bigger context.

ASKED AND ANSWERED

Solomon may have been on a search for the meaning of life, but it appears that he didn't talk to anyone else but himself about it. At least we asked about a thousand other people for their opinions about the meaning of life. But it seems that we weren't the first ones to come up with the idea of presenting the question. Someone else beat us to the punch (another lawyer, wouldn't you know it). We only have evidence that he asked the question of one person, but the individual he asked was imminently qualified to answer.

This lawyer lived about two thousand years ago. We don't have his name, but his story is recorded in the Bible. He put the meaning-of-life question to Jesus. Whether or not you acknowledge Jesus Christ as the Son of God, you'll have to admit—along with the rest of the world—that he is recognized as a wise teacher and prophet. With those credentials, there is probably no one better the lawyer could have asked.

The confrontation between Jesus and the lawyer is recorded in Luke 10:25–28. The religious leaders were trying to trap Jesus in a technicality of Jewish law. All good lawyers ask a question only if they already know the answer, and the lawyer who questioned Jesus was no exception. Here is how the interchange went:

> **Lawyer:** Teacher, what must I do to receive eternal life? [We know he didn't ask "What is the meaning of life?" verbatim, but his question is essentially the same. You can't get more meaningful than knowing the secret to eternal life.]
>
> **Jesus:** What does the law of Moses say? How do you read it?
>
> **Lawyer:** "You must love the Lord your God with all your heart, all your soul, all your strength, and all your mind." And, "Love your neighbor as yourself."
>
> **Jesus:** Right! Do this and you will live.

According to Jesus Christ, love is the threshold principal for finding meaning in life. But Jesus didn't just answer "love" in a generic, amorphous sense. He was very specific and indicated that love must be directed two ways: to God and to others.

HERE IT IS—THE ANSWER YOU HAVE BEEN WAITING FOR
(at least the best we can give you)

We were on to something in Las Vegas when we were ruminating about the role of love in the answer to our question. (We're glad that we didn't come up with findings that contradicted the teachings of Christ. We would hate to be branded as heretics.)

In the introduction to this book, and earlier in this epilogue, we have alluded to the fact that there is no single answer to the meaning of life. We suspect that it is different for every individual. We also suspect that the concept is so complicated and interwoven (to get back to our tapestry metaphor) that no one—especially us—is capable of answering the question definitively in a single statement.

While there is not a solitary answer (at least not one that we can articulate), we definitely heard recurring themes in the answers that people gave to us. We got a sense of these themes from the very start of our trip in Boston, and they continued to arise in our interviews during the remainder of our trip.

To the extent that the findings of our search can be summarized, we conclude that the meaning of life involves the following three elements (drum roll, please):

A LOVE OF GOD

The meaning of life is realized as we love God. By making that statement, we are concurring with Jesus and Solomon. That puts us in pretty good company, but that's not why we mention this factor. We include it, and put it first on the list, because it was so important to so many people.

Many of the people we interviewed were religious. Their particular faiths and denominations varied greatly, but the important role of faith in God was pervasive in their answers.

But a sense of faith was not limited to the replies of religious respondents. Even people who claimed no faith in God gave us answers that included some unending dimension. Religious people used terminology that related meaning to something that had eternal significance. Nonreligious answers included the same sense, but described it in terms like "something that lives beyond me" or "something that will remain after I am gone."

Maybe it isn't surprising that so many people gave answers that included a spiritual aspect. Solomon apparently realized the same thing:

[GOD] HAS PLANTED ETERNITY IN THE HUMAN HEART.
(ECCLESIASTES 3:11)

Based on the responses in our interviews, people have a sense of this eternity, and they know that it is related to finding meaning in life.

A LOVE FOR OTHERS

When replying to the lawyer, Jesus identified two relationships: a vertical one and a horizontal one. The vertical relationship refers to our connection with God. The horizontal relationship refers to our connection with each other. Both relationships require love.

There was more to the story of Jesus and the lawyer than we mentioned above. In an effort to clarify what it meant to "love your neighbor," the lawyer went on to ask Jesus, "Who is my neighbor?" (Those attorneys! Always looking for a loophole.) This is when Jesus told the parable of the Good Samaritan, declaring that everyone is our neighbor and that we have a responsibility to show love to all people.

The answers to our meaning-of-life question had some sense of what Jesus was talking about. They invariably included some connection to other people. Sometimes it was as simple as, "The meaning of life involves being happy for other people's successes." Other times it was described in terms of accomplishments that produce beneficial results for society. Although the jargon differed, the theme was the same. People find meaning in life when they are involved in the lives of others.

A SENSE OF PURPOSE BIGGER THAN YOURSELF

This factor ties into the previous two. Certainly God and others take you beyond yourself. But this factor emphasizes that the other two involve more than just an intellectual acknowledgment of the existence of God and others. A sense of meaning is realized in life when you are actually doing something that benefits others without any selfish motivations.

INTENTIONALITY

Some of the people we talked with didn't have a clue about the meaning of life. We felt sorry for them. Their responses acknowledged that they were adrift in life without any feeling of satisfaction or fulfillment.

Other people expressed some understanding of the elements of the meaning, but they weren't doing anything that integrated those principles into their lives. We felt sorry for those people too. Knowing the secret but not doing anything with it is perhaps more pathetic than not knowing at all.

But we got really excited when we met people who had discovered the meaning of life and had kicked it into gear on a daily basis. We tried to identify a common trait among these people, and it seems to be intentionality. They were intentional about realizing and actualizing the meaning in their lives.

* * *

HENRY DAVID THOREAU SAID THAT "THE MASS OF MEN LEAD LIVES OF QUIET DESPERATION." WE THINK WE MET SOME OF THEM ON OUR SEARCH. A FEW, NOT MANY. MOST OF THE PEOPLE WE MET WERE LIKE US. THEY HAD SOME INKLING ABOUT THE MEANING OF LIFE, BUT THEY WANTED TO GET A BETTER GRASP ON IT. WE SUGGEST A CROSS-COUNTRY TRIP.

For more on our Search for the Meaning of Life (including some fine digital photos) check out our Web site:

www.BRUCEANDSTAN.COM

If you feel like getting in touch, e-mail us at:

GUIDE@BRUCEANDSTAN.COM

Or use our snail mail address:

Bruce & Stan
P.O. Box 25565
Fresno, CA 93729

Either way, we'd love to hear from you!